Publisher 2000 for Windows Workbook Beginners

by Paul Summers

Software Training Workbooks
16 Nursery Road
Pinner
Middlesex
HA5 2AP

ACKNOWLEDGEMENTS

Cover art work by Paul Ostafiehyk @ St. Paul's Reprographics.

ISBN 1-902281-22-5

Published by:
Software Training Workbooks
16 Nursery Road
Pinner
Middlesex
HA5 2AP

Printed by St. Paul's Reprographics, 35 St. Paul's Close, Ealing Common, London, W5 3JQ.

CONTENTS

INTRODUCTION

EXERCISES

INTRODUCTION

TO START PUBLISHER

If you have a menu on the screen follow the instructions to start Publisher 2000.

If you have Windows click on the **Start** button, point at the **Programs** option, then click on the **Microsoft Publisher** option in the programs group.

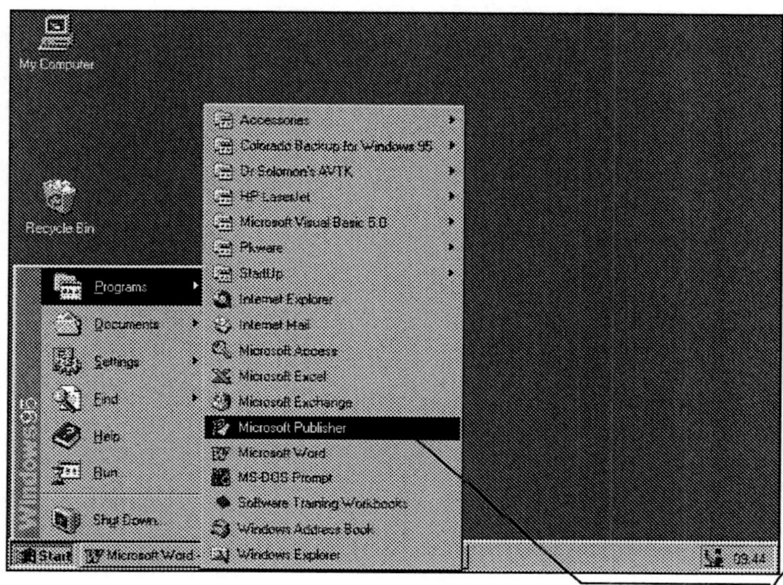

Click the **Microsoft Publisher** option in the Programs group.

Only now should you place your disc in the floppy drive (A:).

OPEN, PRINT & CLEAR A PUBLICATION

Open an existing publication called 'Word for Windows'.

OPEN AN EXISTING PUBLICATION
From the Catalog screen choose the **Publications by Wizard** tab
Click the **Existing Files** button
OR
Select **File** and then **Open**
THEN
Highlight the **3 ½ Floppy (A:)** folder in the Look in box
Type **Word for Windows** in the File name box
Click to **Open** the file
N.B. *You may need to click **OK** again depending on the printer which your machine is connected to.*

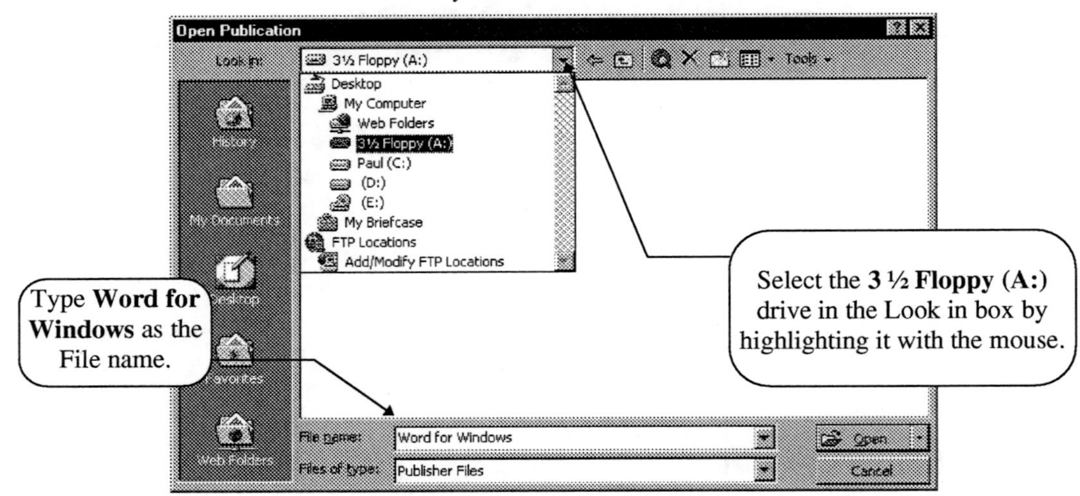

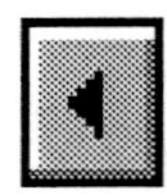

TO BE ABLE TO READ THE TEXT ON THE PUBLICATION
Select **View**, **Zoom**, and then **100%**

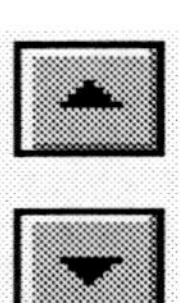

TO SCROLL AROUND THE PUBLICATION
Click on the **Scroll Left/Right** buttons to scroll the screen left or right (see next page)
Click on the **Scroll Up/Down** buttons to scroll the screen up or down (see next page)
Select **View**, **Zoom**, and then **Whole Page**

TO PRINT YOUR PUBLICATION
Select **File** and **Print**
Click the **OK** button to print the page

TO CLEAR THE SCREEN
Select **File** and then **Close**
N.B. *Click **No** if asked to save the changes made.*

TO CLOSE PUBLISHER
Select **File** and then **Exit**

THE PUBLISHER WORKSPACE

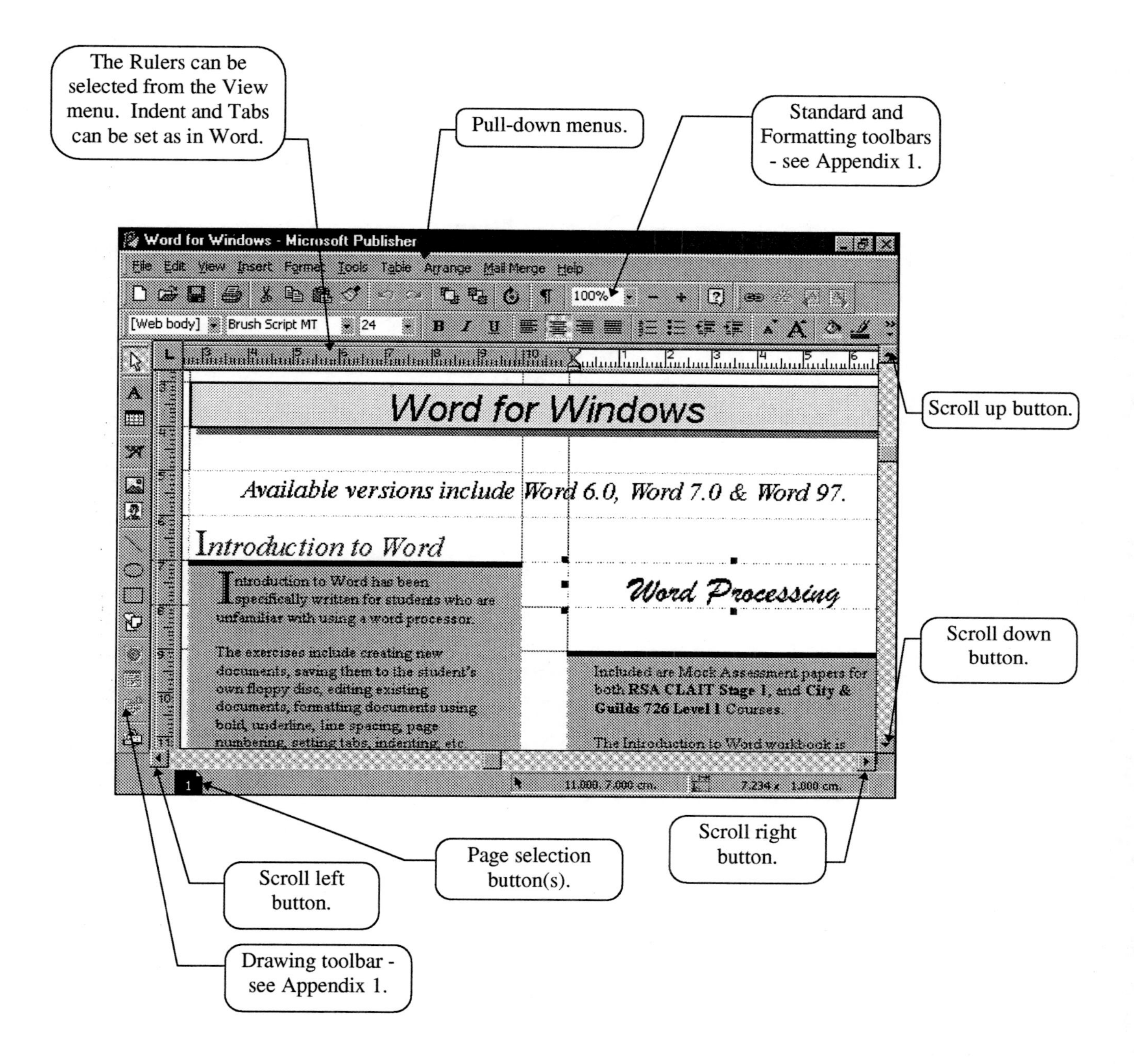

WHAT IS PUBLISHER?

Publisher is a powerful DTP (Desk Top Publishing) package. It can be used to create professional looking publications which combine graphics (pictures, clip art, charts, and drawings) and text.

The range of publications that can be produced include:

- Newsletters
- Brochures
- Flyers
- Business cards
- Business forms
- Letterheads
- Labels
- Postcards
- Signs
- and even Web pages for the Internet

Production of any of the above can be done even by a beginner with the use of Design Wizards - the software lets you choose pre-designed styles (Templates) to which you simply add your text and pictures to produce the finished product.

BASIC CURSOR AND POINTER TYPES

TEXT ENTRY CURSOR

The single-vertical line cursor | indicates the position in a text box at which text can be entered or edited.

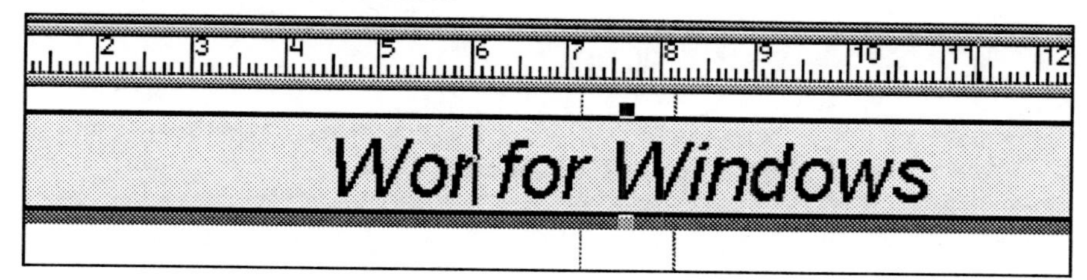

THE I-BEAM POINTER

The I-beam pointer appears where you point the mouse at an object which contains text. **Clicking** with the I-beam pointer will position the text entry cursor at the point selected. **Dragging** with the I-beam pointer will select a block of text.

THE RIGHT (SELECTION) ARROW POINTER

The right arrow pointer appears when you point the mouse to any area of the screen where you can select a command or where you can select an object border such as a text box or a picture frame.

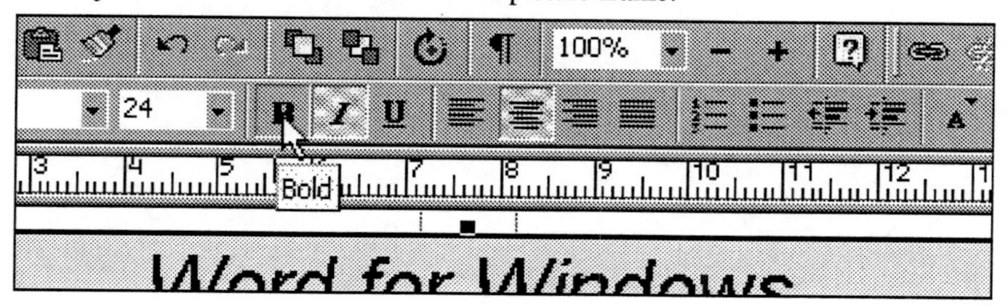

THE MOVE POINTER

When an object is selected it can be moved by **dragging** the side of its frame. The following pointer appears when the move option is available.

MOVE

THE RESIZE POINTER

When an object is selected it can be re-sized by **dragging** one of the handles (boxes) in a corner or on a side of the frame. The following pointers can appear when the re-size option is available.

RESIZE RESIZE RESIZE RESIZE

THE ADJUST POINTER

To position text and graphics accurately it is best to set ruler guides on the page. This can be done by holding down the **Shift** ⇧ key, pointing at the vertical or horizontal ruler, and then **dragging** the Adjust pointer(s). On release of the mouse a ruler guide will be left on the publication.

ADJUST ADJUST

USE HELPFUL POINTERS

The pointers described here will appear if the option **Tools, Options, User Assistance**, and **Use helpful mouse pointers** is ticked ☑.

THE RULER

SWITCHING THE RULER ON

SWITCHING THE RULER ON
Select **View** and tick ☑ the **Rulers** option

INDENTING TEXT WITH THE RULER

The ruler can be used to change the left or right indent setting of a paragraph of text. **Dragging** the Upper Pointer will result in the 1st line of the text indented .

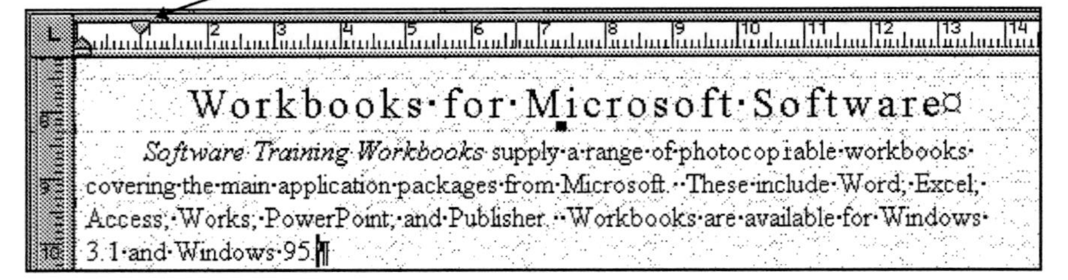

Dragging the Lower Pointer will result in all but the 1st line of the text being indented, this is called hanging indent.

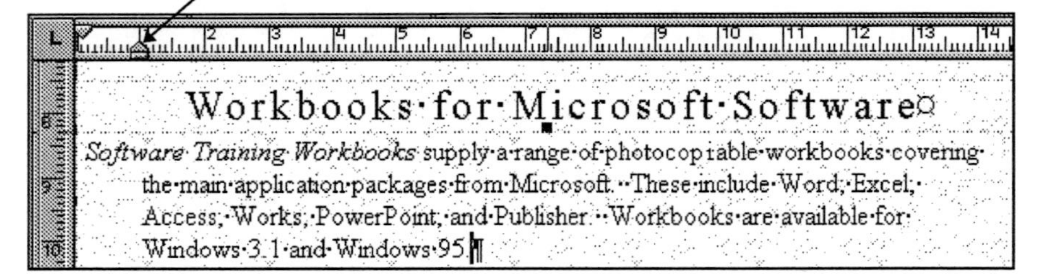

Dragging the bottom Box will result in the entire paragraph being indented.

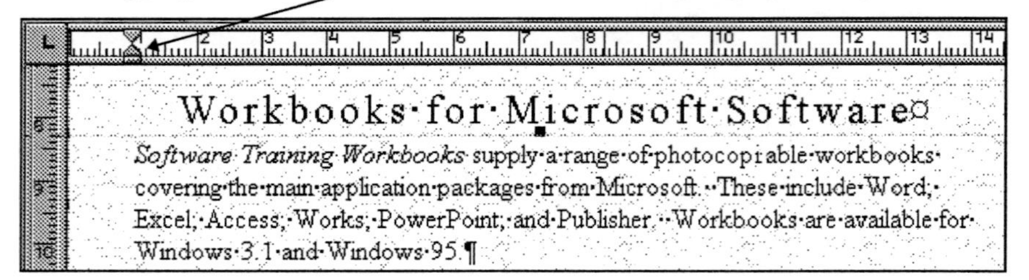

SETTING TABS ON THE RULER

Tabs can be set by simply clicking at the appropriate point on the ruler. The type of tab, Left, Right, Centre, or Decimal can be set by clicking on the Tab selection box to the left of the ruler.

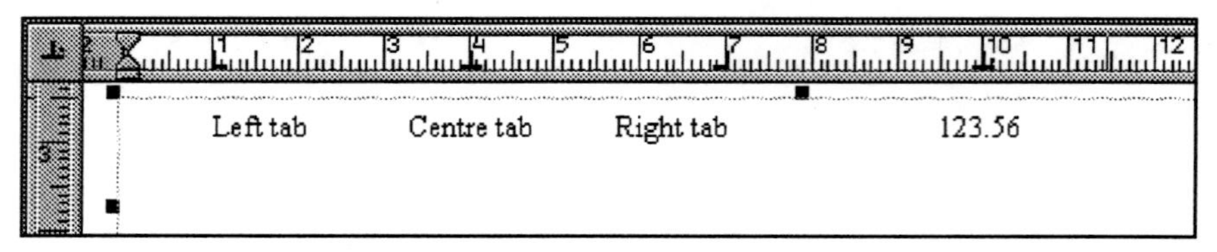

 by Paul Summers

TIPS FOR DESIGNING GOOD PUBLICATIONS

When designing publications there are a number of factors to consider. These include:

- Readability of the publication.
- Attention-grabbing and aesthetic features of the publication.
- What type of message you are trying to put across?
- Who the audience is?

General rules for good publication design include:

- Use large font sizes for headings and sub-headings.
- Do not use more than 2 or 3 different font types.
- Use the Wizards to help in the design of publications.
- Use clip art and graphics wherever possible instead of plain text.

The Templates, Wizards, clip art images, and graphics/table/chart applications built into Publisher are all there to make the design of your publications as easy as possible. Use them.

MOUSE OPERATIONS

To *move* your mouse is to move it without pressing any buttons.

To *select* or *click* is to press the left button and immediately release it without moving the mouse. For example you click on a button to perform some operation.

CLICK
Press the left mouse button.

To *double click* is to press and release the left button twice in rapid succession without moving the mouse.

To *drag* is to press the left button and hold it as you move the mouse. You then release the button to complete the operation. In doing so you invariably *highlight* a piece of text.

DRAG
Press the left mouse button and then move the mouse.

USING THESE EXERCISES

FORMATTING BUTTONS

The Formatting toolbar may not display all the buttons even when an object is highlighted. Click on **More Buttons** if you can not find the button you are looking for.

These exercises have all been written on the assumption that your screen setup is as follows:

- The Word 97-2000 text converter has been installed.
- The paper size is set to A4. Select **File**, **Print**, **Setup**, select Paper Size **A4**, then click **OK**.
- The rulers are ON. To switch on select **View** and tick ☑ the **Rulers** option.
- The measurement system is set to centimetres. To set select **Tools**, **Options**, choose the **General** tab, Measurement units **Centimeters**, and then click **OK**.
- The Standard and Formatting toolbars are in view. To switch on select **View**, **Toolbars**, tick ☑ the **Standard** option and also tick ☑ the **Formatting** option.
- The Snap to Ruler Marks and Snap to Guides options are on. To switch on select **Tools**, tick ☑ **Snap to Ruler Marks** and also tick ☑ **Snap to Guides**.
- The Use helpful pointer option is ON. To set select **Tools**, **Options**, choose the **User Assistance** tab, tick ☑ the **Use helpful mouse pointers** option, and then click **OK**.
- You MUST close down the Office Assistant to access any of the Help menus referred to in this workbook:

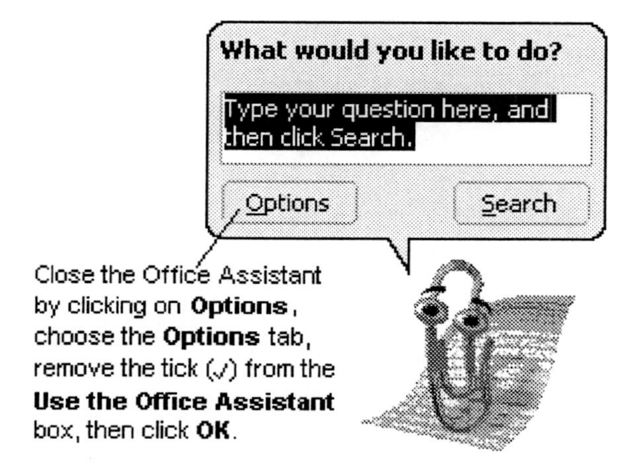

In addition it is assumed that your default page setup is A4 size.

Failure to set the above at the start of each lesson could result in difficulty in some of the exercises in this workbook, so it is advisable to check the above before starting each lesson.

OPENING EXISTING FILES AND SAVING YOUR WORK

Publications that you create new yourself should always be saved on your own disc or allocated area on the file server. The instructions given in these exercises instruct you to save all work on your floppy disc, the 3 ½ Floppy (A:) folder. If you have access to the C: drive or an allocated work area on a network file server you should substitute the instruction to save to the 3 ½ Floppy (A:) folder with the appropriate folder name.

These exercises require at times that you open existing Publisher publications, Word documents, Excel worksheets, and a number of Paint graphics files. These files are then used to build the Publications. The files should be on your disc.

The files required for this workbook are as follows:

Publisher Files:
- Word for Windows

Word Files:
- Art Deco
- Ealing
- Luggage
- New Product Releases
- Winter Sale
- Workbooks

Graphics Files (see Appendix 2):
- Art Deco
- Clock
- Computer User
- Flag
- Graph
- Luggage
- Real Estate

EXERCISE 1

OBJECTIVES

- To use the Help system to learn about Publisher.

INSTRUCTIONS

1. Close the Catalog screen.

   CANCEL THE CATALOG SCREEN
   Select the **Exit Catalog** button in the Catalog screen

2. Use the Tutorial Help system to learn about Publisher.

   USING TUTORIAL HELP
   Select **Help** and **Publisher Tutorials**
   To display this topic, click the graphic
   Click The Basics option **Working with Publisher**
   Read Page 1 of the Tutorial carefully
   Click on the **Page 2** 2 icon and read the Help screen
   Click on **Page 3** to **Page 8** and read the respective Help screens carefully
   Close the Publisher Tutorial Help window

HELP WIZARD

If a Help Wizard window automatically appears on the workspace click the **Hide Wizard** button at the bottom of the screen.

3. Use the Tutorial Help system to learn about layout guides.

   USING TUTORIAL HELP
   Select **Help** and **Publisher Tutorials**
   To display this topic, click the graphic
   Click the Arrange objects on a page option **Working with layout guides**
   Read Page 1 of the Tutorial carefully
   Click on **Page 2** to **Page 6** and read the respective Help screens carefully
   Close the Publisher Tutorial Help window

4. Use the Tutorial Help system to learn about positioning objects.

   USING TUTORIAL HELP
   Select **Help** and **Publisher Tutorials**
   To display this topic, click the graphic
   Click the Arrange objects on a page option **Positioning objects**
   Read Page 1 of the Tutorial carefully
   Click on **Page 2** to **Page 5** and read the respective Help screens carefully
   Close the Publisher Tutorial Help window

EXERCISE 2

OBJECTIVES

- To open a new publication.
- To set the page margin guides of a new publication.
- To create a double-line border along the margins of the publication.
- To save the publication.

INSTRUCTIONS

1. Open a new publication.

   OPENING A NEW PUBLICATION
   Select **File** and then **New**
   THEN/OR
   From the Catalog screen choose the **Blank Publications** tab
   THEN
   Select the type of publication you want to create as a **Full Page** publication (in either the left or right window), and then click **Create**

2. Select **Help**; **Publisher Tutorials**; To display this topic, click the graphic ; click the Arrange objects on a page option **Working with layout guides**. Read Page 1 of the Tutorial carefully. Click on **Page 2** to **Page 6** and read the respective Help screens carefully. **Close** the Publisher Tutorial Help window.

3. Set the page margin guides of the new publication.

   SETTING THE PAGE MARGIN GUIDES
   Select **Arrange**, **Layout Guides**, change the Left, Right, Top and Bottom Margin Guides to **2 cm**, and then click **OK**

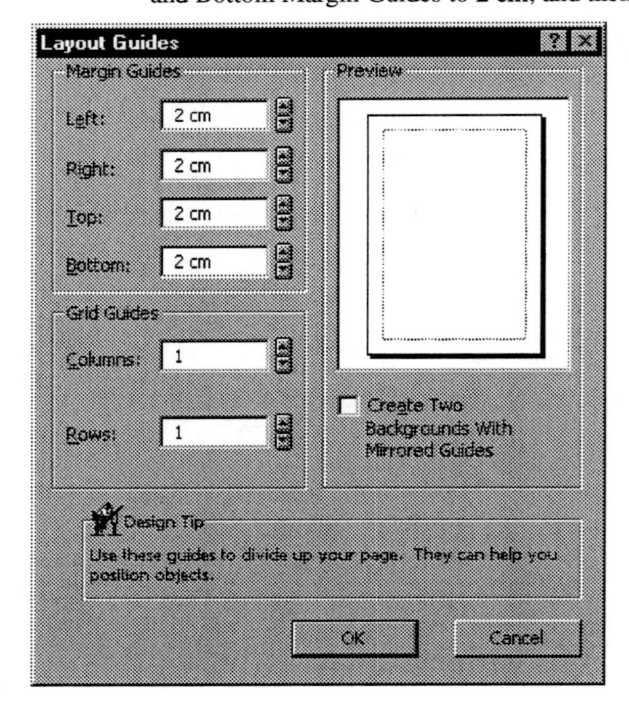

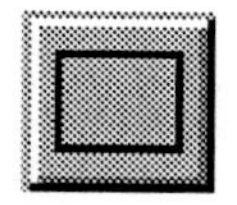

PRINTING PROBLEMS

Do NOT draw either of the boxes OUTSIDE of the margins set. If you do this you will find that you will have printing problems later.

4. Create a double-line border along the margins of the publication.

CREATING A DOUBLE-LINE BORDER
Select **Tools** and place a tick ☑ against **Snap to Guides**
Click the **Rectangle Tool** on the left toolbar, click in the top left (outer) corner margin and hold and **drag** the mouse to the lower right (outer) corner margin to draw the border, select **Format**, **Line/Border Style**, select **More Styles…**, Choose a thickness **4pt**, and then **OK**
Click the **Rectangle Tool** on the left toolbar, click in the top left (inner) corner margin inside the current border and hold and **drag** the mouse to the lower right (inner) corner margin inside the current border to draw the 2nd border, select **Format**, **Line/Border Style**, select **More Styles…**, Choose a thickness **2pt**, and then **OK**

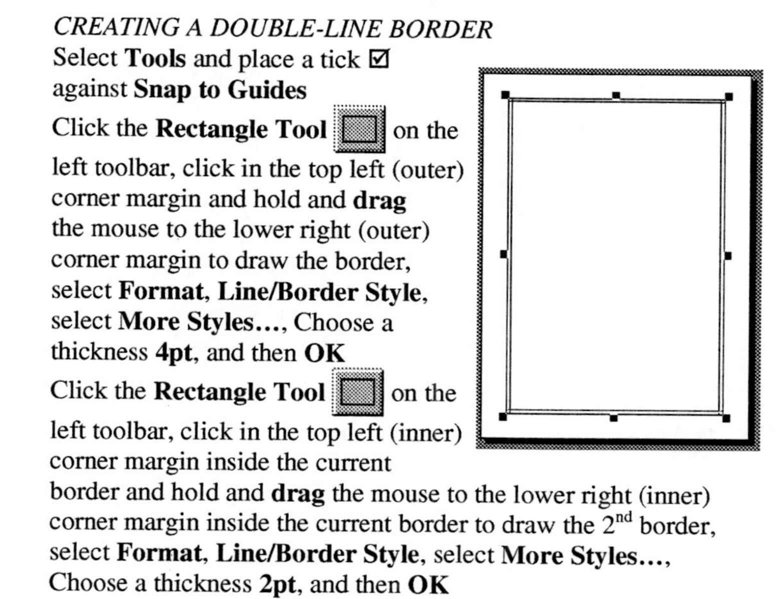

5. Save the publication with the File name 'Double-line border'.

SAVING A PUBLICATION
Select **File** and then **Save**
Select to Save in the **3 ½ Floppy (A:)** folder
Click in the File name box and then enter the name of your publication as **Double-line border**
Click the **Save** button

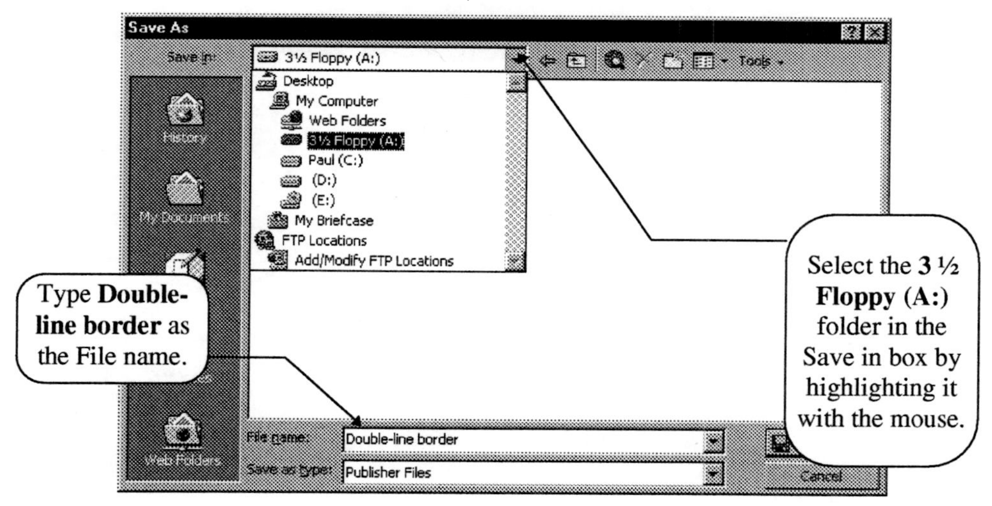

6. Clear the publication by selecting **File** and then **Close**.

EXERCISE 3

OBJECTIVES

- To open an existing publication.
- To create horizontal ruler guides.
- To enter and format text and place it accurately on the page.
- To save the publication with a different name.
- To print a publication.

INSTRUCTIONS

DRIVE

It is important that every time you use this workbook that you set the working folder to the 3 ½ Floppy (A:) drive when opening/saving your work.

1. Open the publication called 'Double-line border'.

   OPEN AN EXISTING PUBLICATION
   From the Catalog screen choose the **Publications by Wizard** tab
   Click the **Existing Files** button
   OR
   Select **File** and then **Open**
   THEN
   Highlight the **3 ½ Floppy (A:)** folder in the Look in box
   Type **Double-line border** in the File name box
   Click to **Open** the file

2. Select **Help**; **Publisher Tutorials**; To display this topic, click the graphic ; click the Arrange objects on a page option **Positioning objects**. Read Page 1 of the Tutorial carefully. Click on **Page 2** to **Page 5** and read the respective Help screens carefully. **Close** the Publisher Tutorial Help window.

3. Create horizontal ruler guides, at 5cm and 10cm from the top of the page in order to help position text accurately on the page.

CREATING HORIZONTAL RULER GUIDES
Select **View** and tick ☑ the **Rulers** option
Hold down the **Shift** [⇧] key and point at the *horizontal* ruler until the **Adjust** pointer appears, click and **drag** the mouse to place a horizontal dashed line on the publication against the **5cm** mark on the *vertical* ruler (release the mouse button)
Hold down the **Shift** [⇧] key and point at the *horizontal* ruler until the **Adjust** pointer appears, click and **drag** the mouse to place a horizontal dashed line on the publication against the **10cm** mark on the *vertical* ruler (release the mouse button)

ADJUST

CO-ORDINATES

The horizontal and vertical position of the pointer is displayed at the bottom of the screen. e.g. 0.00, 5.00cm.

0.000, 5.000 cm.

When the Shift [⇧] key is held down only ONE co-ordinate changes. This is the value appropriate to the guide you are positioning.

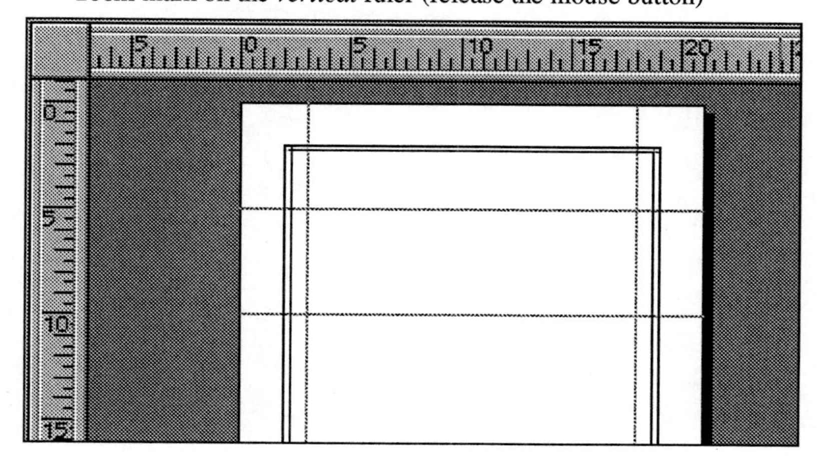

4. Create vertical ruler guides, at 3cm and 18cm from the left of the page, again to help position text accurately on the page.

CREATING VERTICAL RULER GUIDES
Hold down the **Shift** [⇧] key and point at the *vertical* ruler until the **Adjust** pointer appears, click and **drag** the mouse to place a vertical dashed line on the publication against the **3cm** mark on the *horizontal* ruler (release the mouse button)
Hold down the **Shift** [⇧] key and point at the *vertical* ruler until the **Adjust** pointer appears, click and **drag** the mouse to place a vertical dashed line on the publication against the **18cm** mark on the *horizontal* ruler (release the mouse button)

ADJUST

5. Select **Help**; **Microsoft Publisher Help**; choose the **Contents** tab; *double-click* the **Print Publications** book; *double-click* the **Text** book; *double-click* the **Add or replace text** book; *click* **Create a frame and type text in**. Read the Publisher Help screen carefully. **Close** the Publisher Help window.

6. Enter the text 'THE FURNITURE COMPANY', placing it accurately on the page.

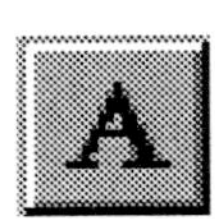

CREATING A TEXT FRAME

Click the **Text Frame Tool** on the left toolbar, click in the top left corner where the **5cm** horizontal guide meets the **3cm** vertical guide and hold and **drag** the mouse to the lower right corner margin where the **10cm** horizontal guide meets the **18cm** vertical guide thus creating a *text frame*

N.B. *If a "Connect Frame" window appears click* **Close**.

FORMATTING AND ENTERING TEXT IN A TEXT FRAME

Select a Font Size **28**pt, click the **Bold** button, click the **Center** text button, type the text

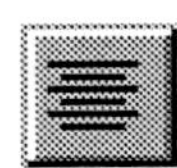

N.B. *Include a space between each character*:

T H E
F U R N I T U R E
C O M P A N Y

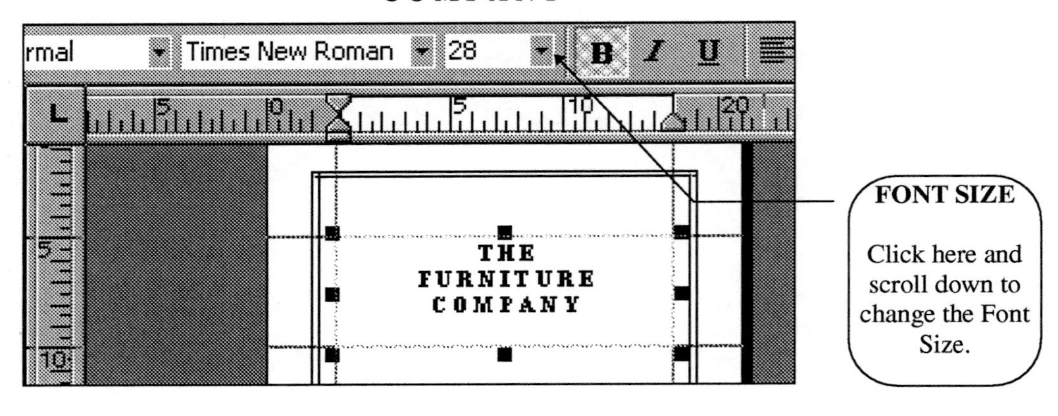

N.B. *Text can ONLY be entered into the text frame when it is highlighted. The appearance of the 8 boxes (handles) around the text frame indicate this. If they disappear draw the frame again or click on where you think it is to select it.*

7. Enter the text 'STOCK REPORT', placing it accurately on the page.

   CREATING HORIZONTAL RULER GUIDES
   Hold down the **Shift** key and point at the *horizontal* ruler until the **Adjust** pointer appears, click and **drag** the mouse to place a horizontal dashed line on the publication against the **20cm** mark on the *vertical* ruler
   Hold down the **Shift** key and point at the *horizontal* ruler until the **Adjust** pointer appears, click and **drag** the mouse to place a horizontal dashed line on the publication against the **22cm** mark on the *vertical* ruler
   CREATING A TEXT FRAME
   Click the **Text Frame Tool** on the left toolbar, click in the top left corner where the **20cm** horizontal guide meets the **3cm** vertical guide and hold and **drag** the mouse to the lower right corner margin where the **22cm** horizontal guide meets the **18cm** vertical guide thus creating a *text frame*
   FORMATTING AND ENTERING TEXT IN A TEXT FRAME
   Select a Font Size **36**pt, click the **Bold** button, click the **Center** text button, type the text **STOCK REPORT**

8. Enter the text 'by Graham Pearson', placing it accurately on the page.

   CREATING HORIZONTAL RULER GUIDES
   Hold down the **Shift** key and point at the *horizontal* ruler until the **Adjust** pointer appears, click and **drag** the mouse to place a horizontal dashed line on the publication against the **22cm** mark on the *vertical* ruler
   Hold down the **Shift** key and point at the *horizontal* ruler until the **Adjust** pointer appears, click and **drag** the mouse to place a horizontal dashed line on the publication against the **25cm** mark on the *vertical* ruler
   CREATING A TEXT FRAME
   Click the **Text Frame Tool** on the left toolbar, click in the top left corner where the **22cm** horizontal guide meets the **3cm** vertical guide and hold and **drag** the mouse to the lower right corner margin where the **25cm** horizontal guide meets the **18cm** vertical guide thus creating a *text frame*
   FORMATTING AND ENTERING TEXT IN A TEXT FRAME
   Select a Font Size **28**pt, click the **Bold** button, click the **Italic** button, click the **Center** text button, type the text:

   by
   Graham Pearson

9. Save the publication with the new name STOCK REPORT.

   SAVING A PUBLICATION WITH A DIFFERENT NAME
   Select **File** and then **Save As**
   Select to Save in the **3 ½ Floppy (A:)** folder
   Click in the File name box and then enter the name of your publication as **STOCK REPORT**
   Click the **Save** button

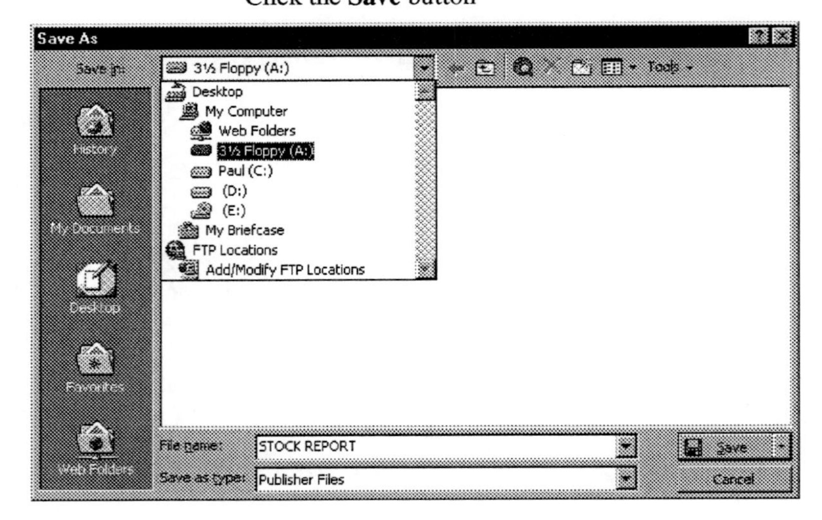

10. **Print** the publication.

11. Clear the publication by selecting **File** and then **Close**.

This text is Times New Roman, 28pt, Bold and Centred.

THE FURNITURE COMPANY

This text is Times New Roman, 36pt, Bold and Centred.

STOCK REPORT

This text is Times New Roman, 28pt, Bold, Italic, and Centred.

by Graham Pearson

EXERCISE 4

OBJECTIVES

- To place a picture accurately on the page.

INSTRUCTIONS

1. Open the publication called 'STOCK REPORT'.

   OPEN AN EXISTING PUBLICATION
   From the Catalog screen choose the **Publications by Wizard** tab
   Click the **Existing Files** button
   OR
   Select **File** and then **Open**
   THEN
   Highlight the **3 ½ Floppy (A:)** folder in the Look in box
   Type **STOCK REPORT** in the File name box
   Click to **Open** the file

2. Select **Help**; **Microsoft Publisher Help**; choose the **Contents** tab; *double-click* the **Print Publications** book; *double-click* the **Pictures** book; *double-click* the **Add a picture** book; *click* **Import a picture from a file**. Read the Publisher Help screen carefully. **Close** the Publisher Help window.

3. Place a picture accurately on the publication.

   CREATING HORIZONTAL RULER GUIDES
   Hold down the **Shift** key and point at the *horizontal* ruler until the **Adjust** pointer appears, click and **drag** the mouse to place a horizontal dashed line on the publication against the **10cm** mark on the *vertical* ruler
   Hold down the **Shift** key and point at the *horizontal* ruler until the **Adjust** pointer appears, click and **drag** the mouse to place a horizontal dashed line on the publication against the **18cm** mark on the *vertical* ruler
   CREATING VERTICAL RULER GUIDES
   Hold down the **Shift** key and point at the *vertical* ruler until the **Adjust** pointer appears, click and **drag** the mouse to place a vertical dashed line on the publication against the **4cm** mark on the *horizontal* ruler

Hold down the **Shift** ⇧ key and point at the *vertical* ruler until the **Adjust** pointer appears, click and **drag** the mouse to place a vertical dashed line on the publication against the **17cm** mark on the *horizontal* ruler

CREATING A PICTURE FRAME

Click the **Picture Frame Tool** on the left toolbar, click in the left corner where the **10cm** horizontal guide meets the **4cm** vertical guide and hold and **drag** the mouse to the lower right corner margin where the **18cm** horizontal guide meets the **17cm** vertical guide thus creating a *picture frame*

INSERTING A PICTURE IN THE FRAME

N.B. *The picture frame must be highlighted - that is the 8 boxes (handles) should be showing.*

Select **Insert**, **Picture**, and then **From File**

Highlight the **3 ½ Floppy (A:)** folder in the Look in box

Type **Real Estate** in the File name box

Click **Insert** to place the picture

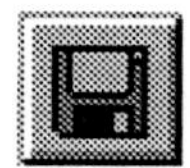

4. **Save** the changes made to the publication.

5. **Print** the publication.

6. Clear the publication by selecting **File** and then **Close**.

THE FURNITURE COMPANY

STOCK REPORT

by

Graham Pearson

EXERCISE 5

OBJECTIVES

- To scale/re-size a picture.
- To make multiple copies of a picture on the same page.
- To save the publication with a different name.

INSTRUCTIONS

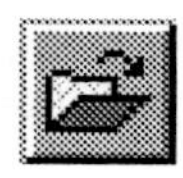

1. **Open** the publication called **STOCK REPORT**.

2. Select **Help**; **Microsoft Publisher Help**; choose the **Contents** tab; *double-click* the **Print Publications** book; *double-click* the **Pictures** book; *double-click* the **Change the look of a picture or picture frame** book; *click* **Resize or crop a picture**. Select the What do you want to do? option **Resize a picture by a specific percentage**. Read the Publisher Help screen carefully. **Close** the Publisher Help window.

3. Scale/re-size the picture.

   TO SCALE AN OBJECT
   Click on the **Real Estate** picture to highlight it (the 8 handles should appear)
   Select **Format** and **Scale Picture**
   N.B. *The Scale Height/Width should both be approx. 200%.*
   Change the Scale height to **100%**
   Change the Scale width to **100%**
   Click **OK** to make the change
   N.B. *Reducing the scale factors by ½ reduces the size to a ¼.*

4. Make multiple copies of the picture on the same page.

   TO COPY AN OBJECT
   Click on the **Real Estate** picture to highlight it (the 8 handles should appear)
   Click the **Copy** button on the toolbar
   Click the **Paste** button on the toolbar
   N.B. *A 2nd copy of the picture should appear on top of the existing one.*
   Point at the new picture and **Move** (click and drag) it to the right of the original

5. Repeat para. 4 above and make two further copies of the Real Estate picture placing them below the existing 2 pictures, in a square group, as shown over the page.

6. Save the publication with the new name STOCK REPORT - RESIZED.

   SAVING A PUBLICATION WITH A DIFFERENT NAME
   Select **File** and then **Save As**
   Select to Save in the **3 ½ Floppy (A:)** folder
   Click in the File name box and then enter the name of your publication as **STOCK REPORT - RESIZED**
   Click the **Save** button

7. **Print** the publication.

8. Clear the publication by selecting **File** and then **Close**.

THE FURNITURE COMPANY

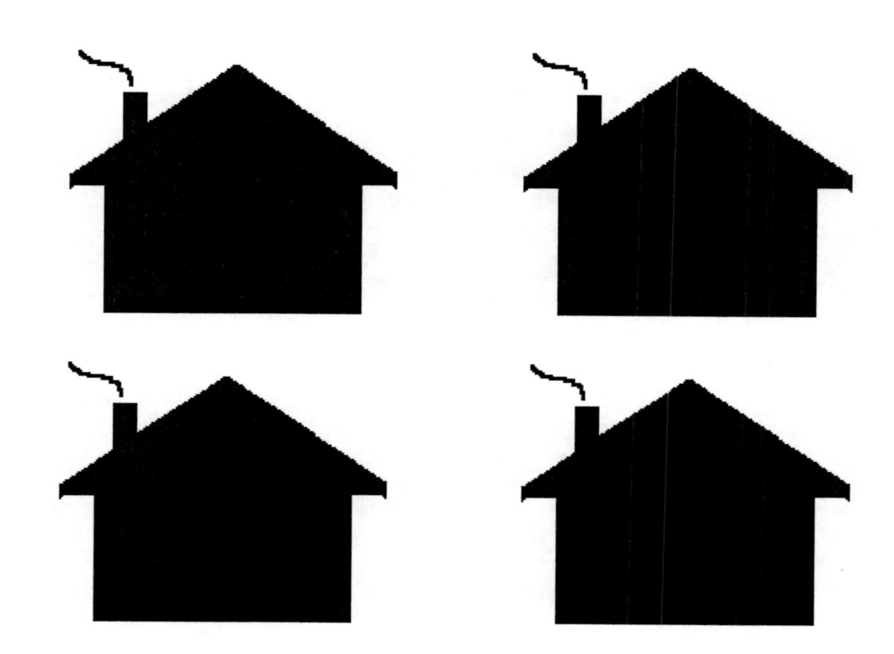

STOCK REPORT

by

Graham Pearson

EXERCISE 6

OBJECTIVES

- To rotate a picture on the page.

INSTRUCTIONS

1. **Open** the publication called **STOCK REPORT - RESIZED.**

2. Select **Help; Publisher Tutorials**; To display this topic, click the graphic ; click the Arrange objects on a page option **Rotating and flipping objects**. Read Page 1 of the Tutorial carefully. Click on **Page 2** to **Page 4** and read the respective Help screens carefully. **Close** the Publisher Tutorial Help window.

3. Rotate a picture (accurately).

   TO USE THE ROTATE POINTER
   Click on the **Real Estate** picture in the *bottom left* corner to highlight it (the 8 handles should appear)

   Hold down the **Alt** [Alt] key, point to one of the handles and when the **Rotate** pointer appears click and **drag** the picture to a new position

   TO USE THE ROTATE BUTTON
   Click on the **Real Estate** picture in the *bottom left* corner

   Click the **Rotate Right** button on the toolbar

   Click the **Rotate Left** button on the toolbar

   TO USE THE ROTATE COMMAND
   Click on the **Real Estate** picture in the *bottom left* corner
   Select **Arrange, Rotate or Flip, Custom Rotate**, set the Angle to **0** and then click **Close**
   N.B. *The picture should now be in its original position.*
   Select **Arrange, Rotate or Flip, Custom Rotate**, set the Angle to **180** and then click **Close**
   N.B. *The picture should now be in its new position which is up-side down.*

4. Repeat para. 3 above for the Real Estate picture in the *bottom right* corner placing it up-side down as well (i.e. **180^0**), as shown over the page.

5. Save the publication with the new name STOCK REPORT - ROTATED.

   SAVING A PUBLICATION WITH A DIFFERENT NAME
   Select **File** and then **Save As**
   Select to Save in the **3 ½ Floppy** (**A:**) folder
   Click in the File name box and then enter the name of your publication as **STOCK REPORT - ROTATED**
   Click the **Save** button

6. **Print** the publication.

7. Clear the publication by selecting **File** and then **Close**.

THE FURNITURE COMPANY

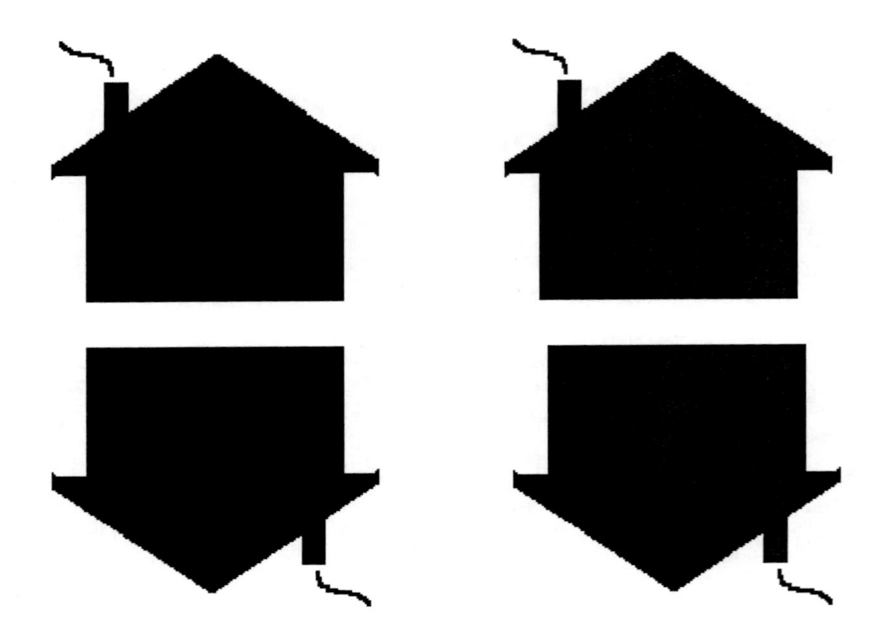

STOCK REPORT

by

Graham Pearson

EXERCISE 7

OBJECTIVES

- To mirror a picture on the page.

INSTRUCTIONS

1. **Open** the publication called **STOCK REPORT - RESIZED.**

2. Select **Help**; **Publisher Tutorials**; To display this topic, click the graphic ; click the Arrange objects on a page option **Rotating and flipping objects**. Read Page 1 of the Tutorial carefully. Click on **Page 2** to **Page 4** and read the respective Help screens carefully. **Close** the Publisher Tutorial Help window.

3. Mirror/flip a picture horizontally.

   TO USE THE MIRROR (FLIP HORIZONTALLY) COMMAND
   Click on the **Real Estate** picture in the *top right* corner
   Click the **Flip Horizontal** button on the toolbar

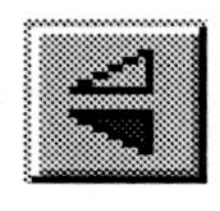

4. Mirror/flip a picture vertically.

   TO USE THE MIRROR (FLIP VERTICALLY) COMMAND
   Click on the **Real Estate** picture in the *bottom left* corner
   Click the **Flip Vertical** button on the toolbar

5. Mirror/flip a picture both horizontally and vertically.

   TO USE THE MIRROR COMMAND
   Click on the **Real Estate** picture in the *bottom right* corner
   Click the **Flip Horizontal** button on the toolbar
   Click the **Flip Vertical** button on the toolbar

6. Save the publication with the new name STOCK REPORT - MIRRORED.

   SAVING A PUBLICATION WITH A DIFFERENT NAME
   Select **File** and then **Save As**
   Select to Save in the **3 ½ Floppy (A:)** folder
   Click in the File name box and then enter the name of your publication as **STOCK REPORT - MIRRORED**
   Click the **Save** button

7. **Print** the publication.

8. Clear the publication by selecting **File** and then **Close**.

THE FURNITURE COMPANY

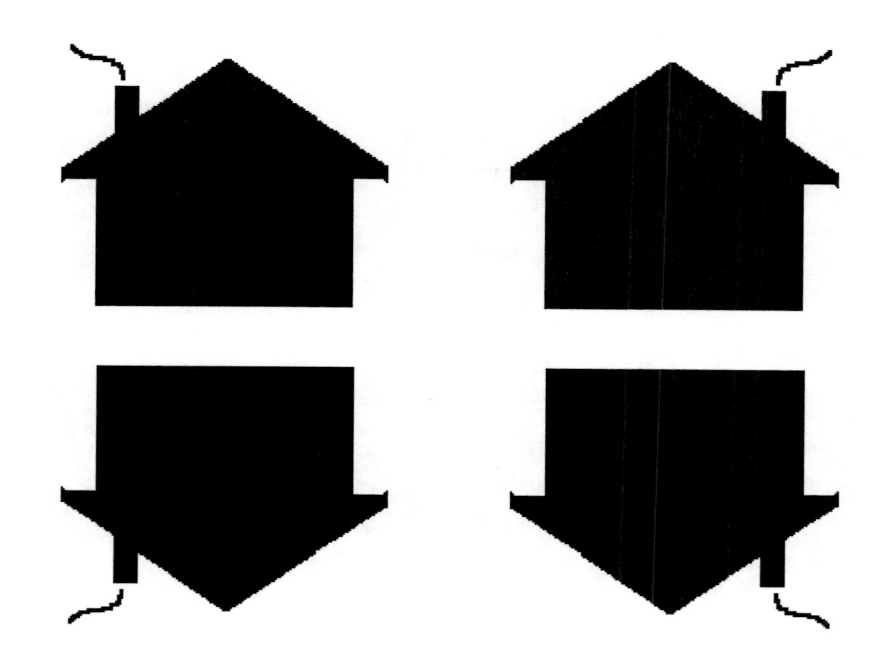

STOCK REPORT

by

Graham Pearson

EXERCISE 8

OBJECTIVES

- To use the crop command to trim a picture.

INSTRUCTIONS

1. **Open** the publication called **STOCK REPORT**.

2. Select **Help**; **Microsoft Publisher Help**; choose the **Contents** tab; *double-click* the **Print Publications** book; *double-click* the **Pictures** book; *double-click* the **Change the look of a picture or picture frame** book; *click* **Resize or crop a picture**. Select the What do you want to do? option **Crop a picture**. Read the Publisher Help screen carefully. **Close** the Publisher Help window.

3. Use the crop command to trim a picture leaving the top left ¼ only.

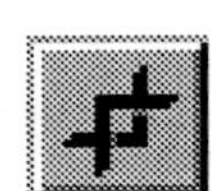

CROPPING A PICTURE
Click on the **Real Estate** picture to highlight it
Click the **Crop Picture** button on the toolbar thus turning the cropping feature ON
Drag the *lower right* handle up to the left with the **Crop** pointer reducing the picture to a ¼ size as shown
Click the **Crop Picture** button on the toolbar thus turning the cropping feature OFF

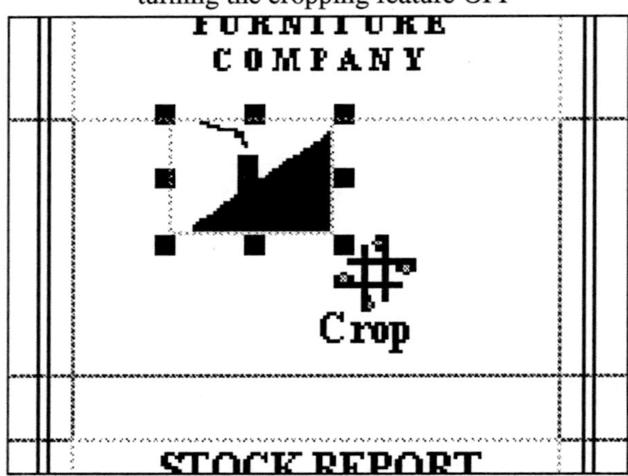

4. Copy a picture.

   TO COPY AN OBJECT
   Click on the *cropped* **Real Estate** picture to highlight it
   Click the **Copy** button on the toolbar
   Click the **Paste** button on the toolbar
   Point at the new picture and **Move** (click and drag) it to the *right* of the original

5. Use the crop command to restore a picture to its original size, and then to crop it again into a different ¼ portion.

   RESTORING A CROPPED PICTURE
   Click on the *cropped* **Real Estate** picture on the *right*
   Click the **Crop Picture** button on the toolbar thus turning the cropping feature ON
   Drag the *lower right* handle down to the right with the **Crop** pointer restoring the picture to its full size
   N.B. *When the full picture is restored it will be partly off the page. This is OK as you will move it back onto the page.*
   CROPPING A PICTURE
   Drag the *lower left* handle up to the right with the **Crop** pointer reducing the picture to a ¼ size as shown
   Click the **Crop Picture** button on the toolbar thus turning the cropping feature OFF
   Point at the new picture and **Move** (click and drag) it to the position shown below

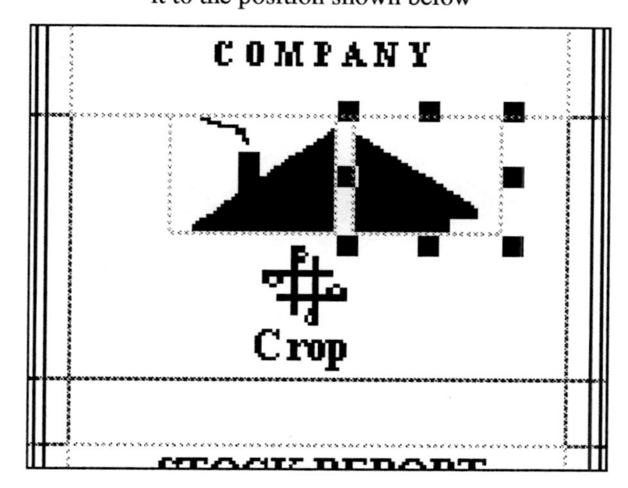

6. Repeat para. 4 and 5 above for the Real Estate picture until there are 4 segments as shown over the page.

7. Save the publication with the new name STOCK REPORT - CROPPED.

   SAVING A PUBLICATION WITH A DIFFERENT NAME
   Select **File** and then **Save As**
   Select to Save in the **3 ½ Floppy (A:)** folder
   Click in the File name box and then enter the name of your publication as **STOCK REPORT - CROPPED**
   Click the **Save** button

8. **Print** the publication.

9. Clear the publication by selecting **File** and then **Close**.

THE FURNITURE COMPANY

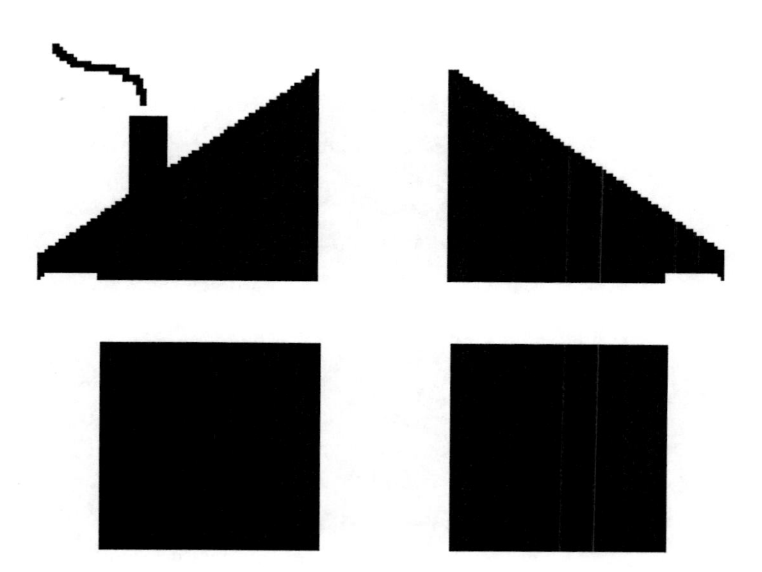

STOCK REPORT

by

Graham Pearson

EXERCISE 9

OBJECTIVES

- To change the colour of a picture.
- To copy a picture from Publisher to Paint and vice versa.
- To edit the picture pixel by pixel in the Paint program.

INSTRUCTIONS

1. **Open** the publication called **STOCK REPORT - RESIZED**.

2. Re-colour each of the 4 Real Estate pictures in Publisher.

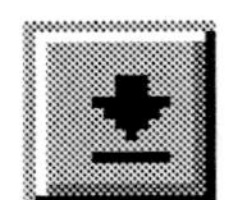

RECOLOUR A PICTURE
Click on the **Real Estate** picture in the *top left* corner
Select **Format**, **Recolor Picture**, click on the **Color** button, click on the **More Colors** button, choose a **Purple** colour, click **OK** and **OK**
Click on the **Real Estate** picture in the *top right* corner
Select **Format**, **Recolor Picture**, click on the **Color** button, click on the **More Colors** button, choose a **Blue** colour, click **OK** and **OK**
Click on the **Real Estate** picture in the *bottom left* corner
Select **Format**, **Recolor Picture**, click on the **Color** button, click on the **More Colors** button, choose a **Green** colour, click **OK** and **OK**
Click on the **Real Estate** picture in the *bottom right* corner
Select **Format**, **Recolor Picture**, click on the **Color** button, click on the **More Colors** button, choose a **Yellow** colour, click **OK** and **OK**

3. Select **Help**; **Microsoft Publisher Help**; choose the **Index** tab; Type keywords **pixels** and click the **search** button; Choose a topic **What is a pixel?** Read the Help window carefully. **Close** the Publisher Help window.

4. Copy a picture from Publisher into Paint.

COPYING A PICTURE TO THE CLIPBOARD
Click on the **Real Estate** picture in the *top left* corner
Click the **Copy** button on the toolbar
PASTING A PICTURE FROM THE CLIPBOARD
Click the **Minimize** button in the top right of the screen to temporarily close down Publisher
Start the **Paint** program *either* from your screen menu *or* from the Programs and Accessories menu
Select **Edit** and then **Paste**
N.B. *The Purple Real Estate picture should be pasted into the Paint program.*

5. Change the colour of the roof and main body of the Real Estate picture in Paint.

USING THE FILL WITH COLOR TOOL

Click the **Fill With Color** button on the left toolbar

Select the **Black** colour in the top left corner of the palette
Click on the **smoke** of the Real Estate picture to in-fill it black
Select the **Dark Grey** colour next to Black in the palette
Click on the Real Estate picture **House** to in-fill it grey

6. Edit the picture pixel by pixel.

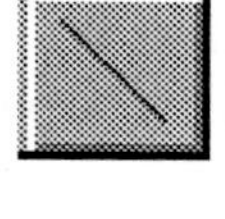

EDITING AN IMAGE PIXEL BY PIXEL
Select **View**, **Zoom**, and then **Large Size**
Select the **White** colour in the bottom left of the palette

Click the button and draw 2 *square windows* in the Real Estate picture as shown

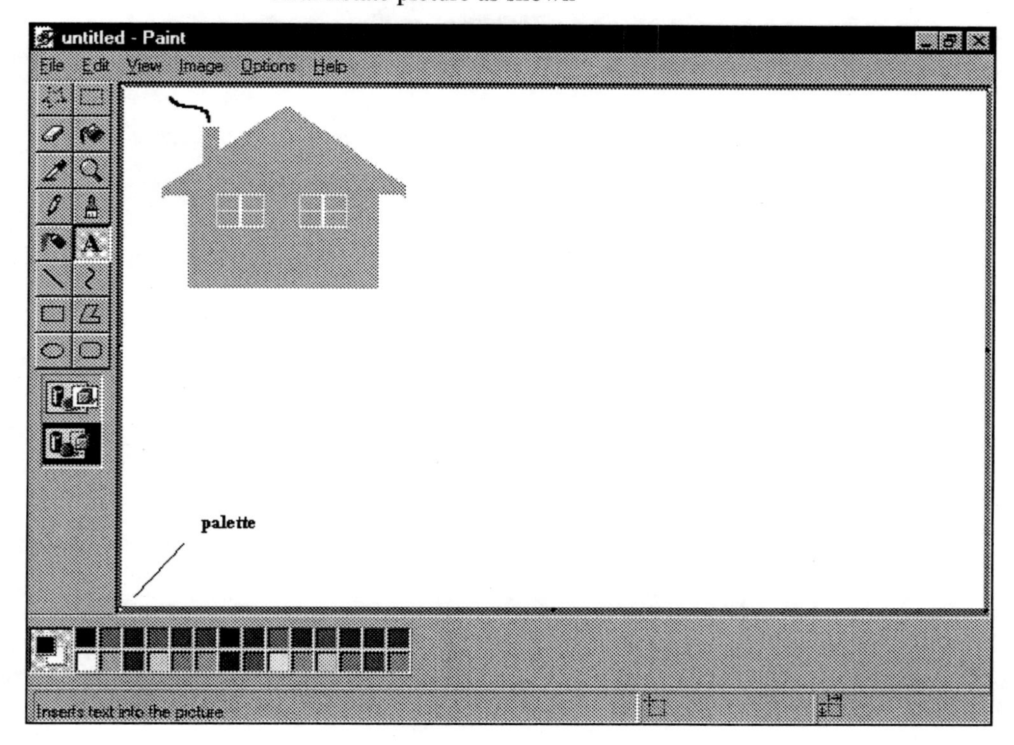

7. Save the Paint file with the name PIXEL.

    SAVING A PAINT FILE
    Select **File** and then **Save**
    Select to Save in the **3 ½ Floppy (A:)** folder
    Click in the File name box and then enter the name of your file as **PIXEL**
    Click the **Save** button

8. Copy the picture from Paint back into Publisher.

    COPYING A PICTURE TO THE CLIPBOARD
    Select **View**, **Zoom**, and then **Normal Size**
    Click the **Select** button on the left toolbar
    Drag the Select pointer from just above the *top left* of the Real Estate picture just below the *bottom right* thus highlighting the picture
    Select **Edit** and then **Copy**
    Clear the Paint screen by selecting **File** and then **New**
    Close the Paint program

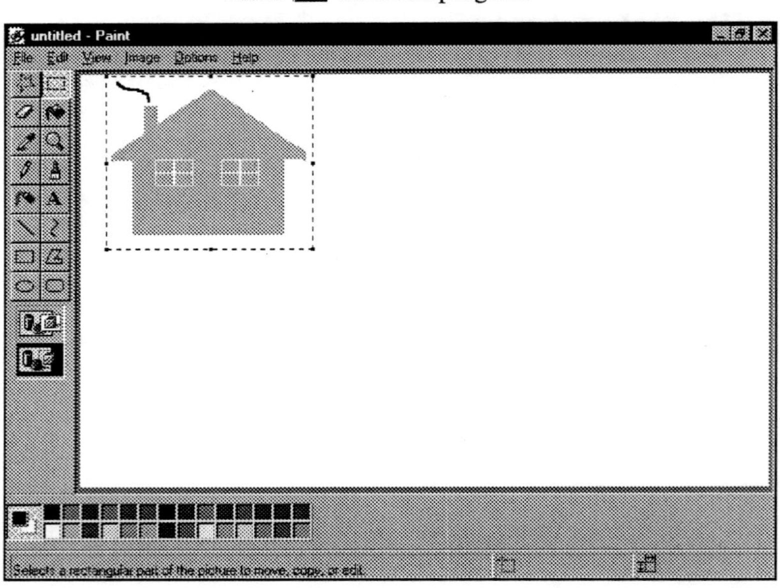

COLOUR CHANGES

The colours you used in Paint may change when pasted into Publisher.

PASTING A PICTURE FROM THE CLIPBOARD
Click the Stock Report... button on the Task toolbar to open up Publisher again
Click on the **Real Estate** picture in the *top left* corner
Click the **Paste** button on the toolbar
N.B. *The modified Real Estate picture should appear.*

9. Save the publication with the new name STOCK REPORT - PIXEL.

   SAVING A PUBLICATION WITH A DIFFERENT NAME
   Select **File** and then **Save As**
   Select to Save in the **3 ½ Floppy (A:)** folder
   Click in the File name box and then enter the name of your publication as **STOCK REPORT - PIXEL**
   Click the **Save** button

10. **Print** the publication.

11. Clear the publication by selecting **File** and then **Close**.

THE FURNITURE COMPANY

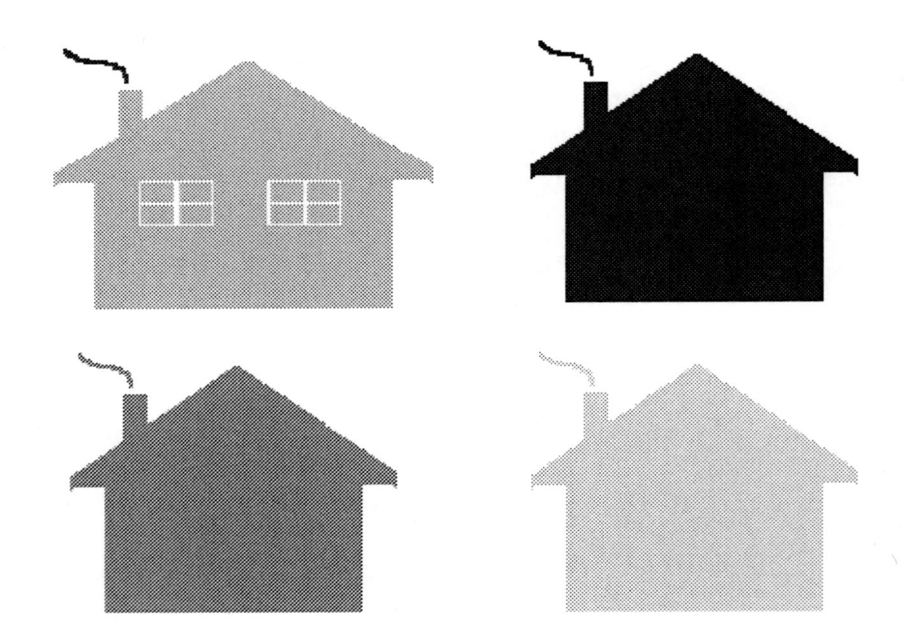

STOCK REPORT

by

Graham Pearson

EXERCISE 10

OBJECTIVES

- To open a new publication.
- To import text in the form of a Word document.
- Adding a Header and a Footer.

INSTRUCTIONS

1. Open a new publication.

   OPENING A NEW PUBLICATION
   Select **File** and then **New**
   THEN/OR
   From the Catalog screen choose the **Blank Publications** tab
   THEN
   Select the type of publication you want to create as a **Full Page** publication (in either the left or right window), and then click **Create**

IMPORTING TEXT

If you are unable to import the Word document into this exercise the Word 97-2000 text converter can be installed from your original application CD.

2. Import text into the publication.

   IMPORTING TEXT
   Click the **Text Frame Tool** A on the left toolbar,
   click in the *top left corner* margin guide and hold and **drag** the mouse to the *lower right corner* margin guide thus creating a single *text frame* for the whole publication
   Select **Insert** and then **Text File**
   Highlight the **3 ½ Floppy (A:)** folder in the Look in box
   Type **EALING** in the File name box
   Click **OK** to insert the file

3. Create horizontal ruler guides at 1cm, 2cm, 27cm and 28cm from the top of the page in order to help position text accurately on the page.

   CREATING HORIZONTAL RULER GUIDES
   Select **View** and **Go to Background**
   Hold down the **Shift** ⇧ key and point at the *horizontal* ruler until the **Adjust** pointer appears, click and **drag** the mouse to place a horizontal dashed line on the publication against the **1cm** mark on the *vertical* ruler
   Repeat the above instructions placing a horizontal ruler guide at **2cm**, **27cm** and **28cm**.

4. Create vertical ruler guides at 2cm and 19cm from the left of the page, again to help position text accurately on the page.

   CREATING VERTICAL RULER GUIDES
   Hold down the **Shift** ⇧ key and point at the *vertical* ruler until the **Adjust** pointer appears, click and **drag** the mouse to place a vertical dashed line on the publication against the **2cm** mark on the *horizontal* ruler
   Repeat the above instructions placing a vertical ruler guide at **19cm**

5. Add a Header and Footer to the publication. N.B. *Headers and footers should be placed on the background of a publication so that they appear on every page - albeit only one page is used here.*

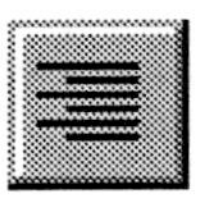

   ADDING A PAGE HEADER TO THE BACKGROUND
   Select **View**, **Zoom**, and then **Whole Page**
   Select **View** and **Go to Background**
   Click the **Text Frame Tool** A on the left toolbar, click in the *top left corner* where the **1cm** horizontal guide meets the **2cm** vertical guide and hold and **drag** the mouse to the where the **2cm** horizontal guide meets the **19cm** vertical guide thus creating a *text frame*
   Select **View**, **Zoom**, and then **100%**
   Click the **Align Right** button, type the text **The Furniture Company**
   ADDING A PAGE FOOTER TO THE BACKGROUND
   Select **View**, **Zoom**, and then **Whole Page**
   Click the **Text Frame Tool** A on the left toolbar, click in the *top left corner* where the **27cm** horizontal guide meets the **2cm** vertical guide and hold and **drag** the mouse to the where the **28cm** horizontal guide meets the **19cm** vertical guide thus creating a *text frame*
   Select **View**, **Zoom**, and then **100%**
   Click the **Align Right** button, type the file name **A:\Ealing**
   Select **View** and **Go to Foreground**

6. Insert the company logo into the top right corner of the publication.

   CREATING A PICTURE FRAME
   Select **View**, **Zoom**, and then **100%**
   Click the **Scroll Up** button move to the top of the page
   With the company address in view on the screen click
   the **Picture Frame Tool** on the left toolbar,
   click in the *top right corner* of the publication and hold and
   drag the mouse to create a *picture frame* approx. **2cm** by **2cm**
   INSERTING A PICTURE IN THE FRAME
   Select **Insert**, **Picture**, and then **From File**
   Highlight the **3 ½ Floppy (A:)** folder in the Look in box
   Type **Real Estate** in the File name box
   Click **Insert** to place the picture

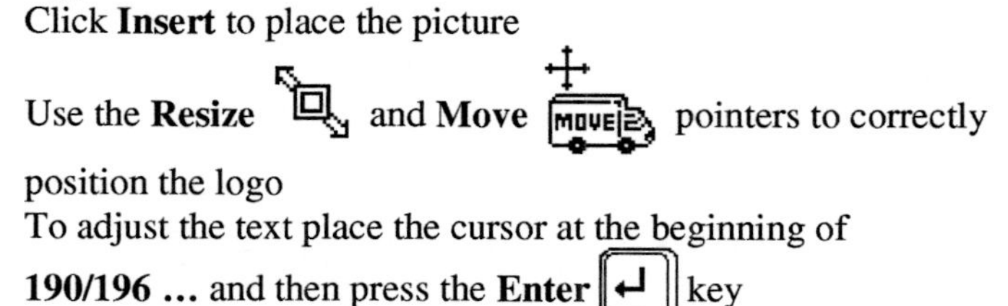

   Use the **Resize** and **Move** pointers to correctly
   position the logo
   To adjust the text place the cursor at the beginning of
   190/196 ... and then press the **Enter** key

7. Save the publication with the File name EALING.

   SAVING A PUBLICATION
   Select **File** and then **Save**
   Select to Save in the **3 ½ Floppy (A:)** folder
   Click in the File name box and then enter the name of
   your publication as **EALING**
   Click the **Save** button

8. **Print** the publication.

9. Clear the publication by selecting **File** and then **Close**.

THE FURNITURE COMPANY

The Furniture Company

190/196 The High Street
Willesden
London
NW10 3XD
Tel: 0181 459 0011

18/04/98
Our Ref: PB/ACH

Ealing Furniture Ltd
11 Broadway Buildings
Boston Road
London
W7

Dear Mr Kane

YOUR ORDER - CARPENTER'S WALL CLOCK

Thank you for your recent order for 20 Carpenter's Wall Clocks, Stock Code 256/1712 @ £56.99 each, which we received today. We regret that due to unforeseen demand for the above named item we are currently out of stock. We have placed an order with our suppliers and they will deliver late next week. We will despatch the items to you immediately they arrive.

We trust that this delay will not inconvenience you and we look forward to your custom in the future.

Yours sincerely

Mrs P Baxter
Sales Manager

A:\Ealing

EXERCISE 11

OBJECTIVES

- To open a new publication.
- To import text in the form of a Word document.
- To draw lines on the publication.

INSTRUCTIONS

1. Open a new publication.

   OPENING A NEW PUBLICATION
   Select **File** and then **New**
   THEN/OR
   From the Catalog screen choose the **Blank Publications** tab
   THEN
   Select the type of publication you want to create as a **Full Page** publication (in either the left or right window), and then click **Create**

2. Set the page margin guides of the new publication.

   SETTING THE PAGE MARGIN GUIDES
   Select **Arrange**, **Layout Guides**, change the Left, Right, Top and Bottom Margin Guides to **2 cm**, and then click **OK**

3. Create horizontal ruler guides, at 2cm, 4cm, 6cm, 8cm, 9cm, 18cm, 19cm, 21cm and 27cm from the top of the page in order to help position text accurately on the page.

   CREATING HORIZONTAL RULER GUIDES
   Select **View** and tick ☑ the **Rulers** option
   Hold down the **Shift** ⇧ key and point at the *horizontal* ruler until the **Adjust** pointer appears, click and **drag** the mouse to place a horizontal dashed line on the publication against the **2cm** mark on the *vertical* ruler
   Repeat the above instructions placing horizontal ruler guides at **4cm**, **6cm**, **8cm**, **9cm**, **18cm**, **19cm**, **21cm** and **27cm**

4. Create vertical ruler guides at 2cm, 15cm and 19cm from the left of the page, again to help position text accurately on the page.

   CREATING VERTICAL RULER GUIDES
   Hold down the **Shift** ⇧ key and point at the *vertical* ruler until the **Adjust** pointer appears, click and **drag** the mouse to place a vertical dashed line on the publication against the **2cm** mark on the *horizontal* ruler
   Repeat the above instructions placing vertical ruler guides at **15cm** and **19cm**

5. Enter the text 'THE FURNITURE COMPANY - Taking care of your needs', placing it accurately on the page.

   CREATING A TEXT FRAME
   Click the **Text Frame Tool** [A] on the left toolbar,
   click in the *top left corner* where the **2cm** horizontal guide meets the **2cm** vertical guide and hold and **drag** the mouse to where the the **4cm** horizontal guide meets the **15cm** vertical guide thus creating a *text frame*
   FORMATTING AND ENTERING TEXT IN A TEXT FRAME
   Select **View**, **Zoom**, and then **100%**
   Select a Font type **Arial**, Font Size **22**pt, click the **Bold** [B] button, type the text **THE FURNITURE COMPANY**, press the **Enter** [↵] key for a new line
   Select a Font type **Times New Roman**, Font Size **18**pt, click the **Italic** [I] button, type the text **Taking care of your needs**
   Select **View**, **Zoom**, and then **Whole Page**

6. Draw lines, of thickness 2pt, on the top and bottom of the entered text.

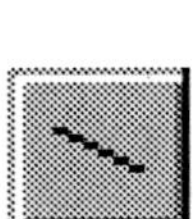

   DRAWING LINES
   Click the **Line** button on the left (drawing) toolbar,
   click where the **2cm** horizontal guide meets the **2cm** vertical guide and hold and **drag** the mouse to where the **2cm** horizontal guide meets the **15cm** vertical guide thus drawing a line *above* the entered text, select **Format**, **Line/Border Style**, select **More Styles...**, select Line thickness **2pt**, and then **OK**
   Click the **Line** button on the left (drawing) toolbar,
   click where the **4cm** horizontal guide meets the **2cm** vertical guide and hold and **drag** the mouse to where the **4cm** horizontal guide meets the **15cm** vertical guide thus drawing a line *below* the entered text, select **Format**, **Line/Border Style**, select **More Styles...**, select Line thickness **2pt**, and then **OK**

7. Enter the text 'WINTER SALE', placing it accurately on the page.

   CREATING A TEXT FRAME
   Click the **Text Frame Tool** [A] on the left toolbar,
   click in the left corner where the **6cm** horizontal guide meets the **2cm** vertical guide and hold and **drag** the mouse to where the the **8cm** horizontal guide meets the **19cm** vertical guide thus creating a *text frame*
   FORMATTING AND ENTERING TEXT IN A TEXT FRAME
   Select a Font type **Arial**, Font Size **36**pt, click the **Bold** [B] button, click the **Center** button, type the text **W I N T E R S A L E** including spaces between each character

8. Import text into the publication.

IMPORTING TEXT
Click the **Text Frame Tool** on the left toolbar,
click in the left corner where the **9cm** horizontal guide meets the **2cm** vertical guide and hold and **drag** the mouse to where the the **18cm** horizontal guide meets the **19cm** vertical guide thus creating a *text frame*
Select **Insert** and then **Text File**
Highlight the **3 ½ Floppy (A:)** folder in the Look in box
Type **WINTER SALE** in the File name box
Click **OK** to insert the file
FORMATTING THE IMPORTED TEXT
Select **View**, **Zoom**, and then **100%**
Select **Edit** and **Highlight Entire Story**, change the Font Size to **12**pt
Drag the I-beam pointer across the text **Discounted items include** to highlight the text, click the **Italic** button
Drag the I-beam pointer across the text **A wide range of ...** down to **D-I-Y tools** to highlight the 4 lines of text, click the **Bullets** button
Drag the I-beam pointer across the text **A wide range of ...** down to **D-I-Y tools** to highlight the 4 lines of text, **drag** the bottom Indent box to the **4cm** mark on the ruler
Select **View**, **Zoom**, and then **Whole Page**

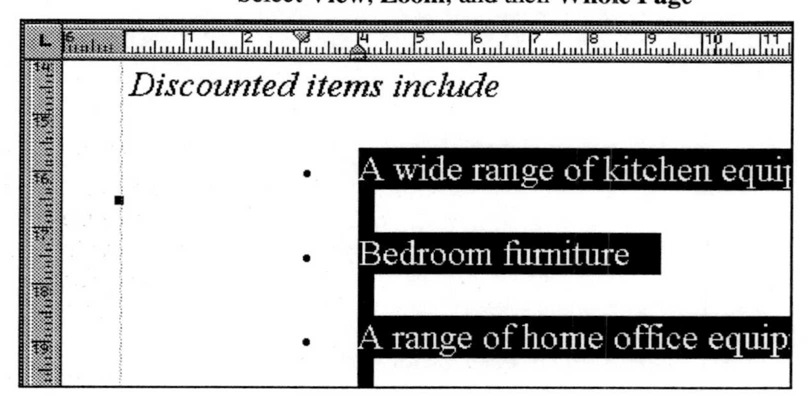

9. Draw a line, of thickness 8pt, across the publication.

DRAWING A LINE
Click the **Line** button on the left toolbar,
click where the **19cm** horizontal guide meets the **2cm** vertical guide and hold and **drag** the mouse to where the **19cm** horizontal guide meets the **19cm** vertical guide thus drawing a line,
select **Format**, **Line/Border Style**, select **More Styles...**,
select Line thickness **8pt**, and then **OK**

10. Enter the remaining text 'SALE COMMENCES ..... Tel: 0181 459 0011', placing it accurately on the page.

    CREATING A TEXT FRAME
    Click the **Text Frame Tool** [A] on the left toolbar,
    click in the left corner where the **21cm** horizontal guide meets the **2cm** vertical guide and hold and **drag** the mouse to where the the **27cm** horizontal guide meets the **19cm** vertical guide thus creating a *text frame*
    FORMATTING AND ENTERING TEXT
    Type the following text with the styles as shown over the page

SALE COMMENCES
9.00am Saturday 1st of December

Don't be late!

190/196 The High Street, Willesden, London, NW10 3XD.
Tel: 0181 459 0011.

11. Insert the company logo into the top right corner of the publication.

    CREATING A PICTURE FRAME
    Select **View**, **Zoom**, and then **100%**
    Click the **Scroll Up** button move to the top of the page
    Click the **Picture Frame Tool** on the left toolbar, click in the *top right* corner where the **2cm** horizontal guide meets the **15cm** vertical guide and hold and **drag** the mouse to where the the **4cm** horizontal guide meets the **19cm** vertical guide thus creating a *picture frame*
    INSERTING A PICTURE IN THE FRAME
    Select **Insert**, **Picture**, and then **From File**
    Highlight the **3 ½ Floppy (A:)** folder in the Look in box
    Type **Real Estate** in the File name box
    Click **Insert** to place the picture

12. Save the publication with the File name WINTER SALE.

    SAVING A PUBLICATION
    Select **File** and then **Save**
    Select to Save in the **3 ½ Floppy (A:)** folder
    Click in the File name box and then enter the name of your publication as **WINTER SALE**
    Click the **Save** button

13. **Print** the publication.

14. Clear the publication by selecting **File** and then **Close**.

Arial, 22pt and Bold.

THE FURNITURE COMPANY

Times, 18pt, & Italic.

Taking care of your needs

Arial, 36pt, Bold, Centred with character spacing.

W I N T E R   S A L E

Times, 12pt.

Here at The Furniture Company you will find hundreds of branded products at cut prices in our Winter Sale. We have specially selected products from our catalogue and cut their prices so that you can buy some real bargains. But hurry because at these low prices some bargains may not last too long and the sale must end on the 21st of December.

Don't forget that our new catalogue is available from the 12th of December.

Italic.

Discounted items include

Bullets with a 2.5cm Indent & Double line spacing.

- A wide range of kitchen equipment
- Bedroom furniture
- A range of home office equipment and furniture
- D-I-Y tools

Times, 18pt, Bold & Centred.

SALE COMMENCES
9.00am Saturday 1st of December

Times, 18pt, Bold, Centred & Italic.

Don't be late!

Times, 12pt, Bold & Centred.

190/196 The High Street, Willesden, London, NW10 3XD.
Tel: 0181 459 0011.

EXERCISE 12

OBJECTIVES

- To open a new publication.
- To create white text on a black background.

INSTRUCTIONS

DISC FULL

Your disc could be nearly full at this stage so it would be a good idea to delete some of the files you have completed - copy them to another disc first.

1. Open a new publication.

   OPENING A NEW PUBLICATION
   Select **File** and then **New**
   THEN/OR
   From the Catalog screen choose the **Blank Publications** tab
   THEN
   Select the type of publication you want to create as a **Full Page** publication (in either the left or right window), and then click **Create**

2. Set the page margin guides of the new publication.

   SETTING THE PAGE MARGIN GUIDES
   Select **Arrange**, **Layout Guides**, change the Left, Right, Top and Bottom Margin Guides to **1 cm**, and then click **OK**

3. Create horizontal ruler guides at 1cm, 4cm, 5cm and 28cm from the top of the page in order to help position text accurately on the page.

   CREATING HORIZONTAL RULER GUIDES
   Select **View** and tick ☑ the **Rulers** option
   Hold down the **Shift** ⇧ key and point at the *horizontal* ruler until the **Adjust** pointer appears, click and **drag** the mouse to place a horizontal dashed line on the publication against the **1cm** mark on the *vertical* ruler
   Repeat the above instructions to place horizontal ruler guides at the **4cm**, **5cm** and **28cm** marks

4. Create vertical ruler guides at 1cm and 20cm from the left of the page, again to help position text accurately on the page.

   CREATING VERTICAL RULER GUIDES
   Hold down the **Shift** ⇧ key and point at the *vertical* ruler until the **Adjust** pointer appears, click and **drag** the mouse to place a vertical dashed line on the publication against the **1cm** mark on the *horizontal* ruler
   Repeat the above instructions to place a vertical ruler guide at the **20cm** mark

FORMATTING BUTTONS

The Formatting toolbar may not display all the buttons even when an object is highlighted. Click on **More Buttons**  if you can not find the button you are looking for.

5. Enter the text 'The FURNITURE COMPANY New product releases', placing it accurately on the page.

   CREATING A TEXT FRAME
   Click the **Text Frame Tool** on the left toolbar,
   click in the left corner where the **1cm** horizontal guide meets the **1cm** vertical guide and hold and **drag** the mouse to where the the **4cm** horizontal guide meets the **20cm** vertical guide thus creating a *text frame*
   FORMATTING AND ENTERING TEXT
   Click the **Bold** and **Center** buttons, select a Font Size **36**pt, click the **Italic** button, type the text **The**, click the **Italic** button again, type the text **FURNITURE COMPANY**, press **Enter** key for a new line
   Select a Font Size **20**pt, type the text **New product releases**
   WHITE TEXT ON A BLACK BACKGROUND
   Click the **Fill Color** button and choose the **Black** colour on the palette
   N.B. *The text will now disappear.*
   Select **Edit** and **Highlight Entire Story**, click the **Font Color** button and choose the **White** colour on the palette

6. Save the publication with the File name NEW PRODUCT RELEASES.

   SAVING A PUBLICATION
   Select **File** and then **Save**
   Select to Save in the **3 ½ Floppy (A:)** folder
   Click in the File name box and then enter the name of your publication as **NEW PRODUCT RELEASES**
   Click the **Save** button

7. **Print** the publication.

8. Clear the publication by selecting **File** and then **Close**.

The FURNITURE COMPANY

New product releases

EXERCISE 13

OBJECTIVES

- To import text from a Word publication.
- To use styles to enhance the imported text.

INSTRUCTIONS

1. **Open** the publication called **NEW PRODUCT RELEASES**.

2. Import text into the publication.

    IMPORTING TEXT
    Click the **Text Frame Tool** **A** on the left toolbar,
    click in the left corner where the **5cm** horizontal guide meets the **1cm** vertical guide and hold and **drag** the mouse to where the the **28cm** horizontal guide meets the **20cm** vertical guide thus creating a *text frame*
    Select **Insert** and then **Text File**
    Highlight the **3 ½ Floppy (A:)** folder in the Look in box
    Type **NEW PRODUCT RELEASES** in the File name box
    Click **OK** to insert the file

3. Create a 'Section Heading' style for use in the current publication.

    CREATING STYLES
    Select **Format**, **Text Style**, Click to **Create a new style**, Enter new style name **Main Heading**, Click to change **Character type and size**, choose a Font **Arial**, choose Size **14pt** and Font style **Bold**, then click **OK**, and **OK**, and then **Close** to create the style

STYLES

A style is a number of font attributes (e.g. Bold, 14pt size, Arial font) which a given piece of text is formatted to. The 'style' can be applied to any text in the publication.

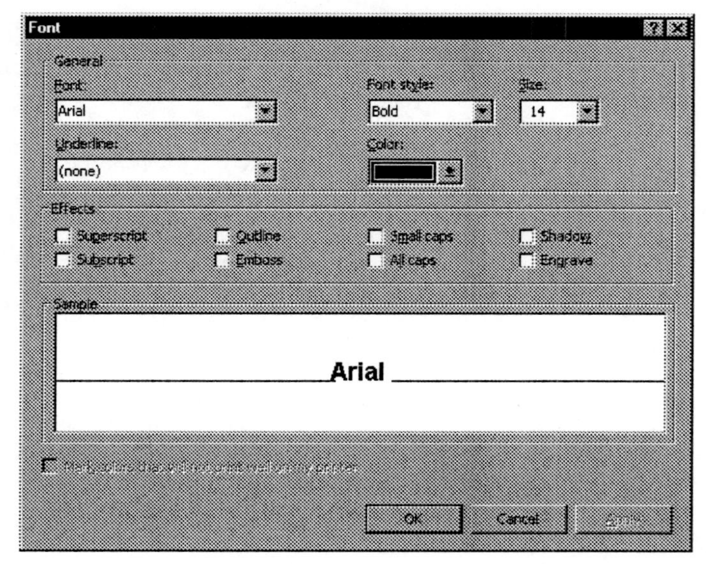

4. Apply the Main Heading style to enhance part of the imported text.

   APPLYING STYLES
   Select **View**, **Zoom**, and then **100%**
   Drag the I-beam pointer across the text **NEW PRODUCTS** to highlight it
   Choose the Style **Main Heading**

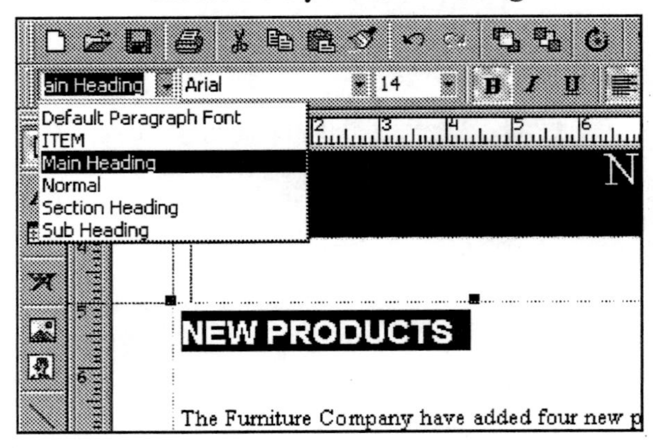

5. Create a 'Section Heading' style for use in the current publication.

   CREATING STYLES
   Select **Format**, **Text Style**, Click to **Create a new style**, Enter new style name **Section Heading**, Click to change **Character type and size**, choose a Font **Arial**, choose Size **12**pt and Font style **Bold**, then click **OK**, and **OK**, and then **Close** to create the style

6. Apply the Section Heading style to enhance parts of the imported text. N.B. *Do NOT highlight the text in the table immediately below the main heading 'NEW PRODUCTS' but rather the individual headings lower down.*

   APPLYING STYLES
   Drag the I-beam pointer across the heading **STOCK ITEM - 256/1712** to highlight it (see page 46)
   Choose the Style **Section Heading**
   Drag the I-beam pointer across the heading **STOCK ITEM - 600/2095** to highlight it
   Choose the Style **Section Heading**
   Drag the I-beam pointer across the heading **STOCK ITEM - 645/1732** to highlight it
   Choose the Style **Section Heading**
   Drag the I-beam pointer across the heading **STOCK ITEM - 645/1749** to highlight it
   Choose the Style **Section Heading**

7. Create a 'Sub Heading' style for use in the current publication.

    CREATING STYLES
    Select **Format**, **Text Style**, Click to **Create a new style**, Enter new style name **Sub Heading**, Click to change **Character type and size**, choose a Font **Times New Roman**, choose Size **10**pt and Font style **Italic**, then click **OK**, and **OK**, and then **Close** to create the style

8. Apply the Sub Heading style to enhance parts of the imported text. N.B. *Do NOT highlight the text in the table immediately below the main heading 'NEW PRODUCTS' but rather the individual headings lower down.*

    APPLYING STYLES
    Drag the I-beam pointer across the text **The Carpenter's Wall Clock** to highlight it (see page 46)
    Choose the Style **Sub Heading**
    Drag the I-beam pointer across the text **The Pine Kitchen Table** to highlight it
    Choose the Style **Sub Heading**
    Drag the I-beam pointer across the text **The Lounge Unit in Black Ash** to highlight it
    Choose the Style **Sub Heading**
    Drag the I-beam pointer across the text **The Lounge Unit in Mahogany** to highlight it
    Choose the Style **Sub Heading**

9. **Save** the changes made to the publication.

10. **Print** the publication.

11. Clear the publication by selecting **File** and then **Close**.

The FURNITURE COMPANY

New product releases

NEW PRODUCTS ← *Main Heading*

The Furniture Company have added four new products to its catalogue for the year commencing October 1998. These are as follows:

256/1712 Carpenter's Wall Clock
600/2095 Pine Kitchen Table
645/1732 Lounge Unit in Black Ash
645/1749 Lounge Unit in Mahogany

All four items are keenly priced against similar products by our major competitors and we feel that you will find that they will sell well.

STOCK ITEM - 256/1712 ← *Section Heading*

The Carpenter's Wall Clock. ← *Sub Heading*

The Carpenter's Wall Clock is available in a range of different colours to suite all available tastes and environments.

The internal mechanisms are made to the highest standards with a Quartz crystal that is accurate to one second error every 10 years.

STOCK ITEM - 600/2095

The Pine Kitchen Table.

This solid pine kitchen table is available in both natural and antique finishes. A unique anti-scratch lacquer only available to The Furniture Company protects the surface.

This fine table can also be purchased with a set of matching chairs and would look at home in any dining room in the land.

STOCK ITEM - 645/1732

The Lounge Unit in Black Ash.

The Lounge Unit has a range of features that include four deep drawers and adjustable shelving which can vary from 6" to 20" in height. With its black ash textured finish this unit can be matched with the furnishings in most modern homes.

STOCK ITEM - 645/1749

The Lounge Unit in Mahogany.

This unit is the same as item 645/1732 as detailed above except that the finish is mahogany veneer. This unit has the same adjustable shelf features as the Lounge Unit in Black Ash.

EXERCISE 14

OBJECTIVES

- To create columns of text.
- To use leading to adjust the spacing between lines of text.

INSTRUCTIONS

1. **Open** the publication called **NEW PRODUCT RELEASES**.

2. Create vertical ruler guides at 10cm and 11cm from the left of the page.

   CREATING VERTICAL RULER GUIDES
   Hold down the **Shift** ⇧ key and point at the *vertical* ruler until the **Adjust** pointer appears, click and **drag** the mouse to place a vertical dashed line on the publication against the **10cm** mark on the *horizontal* ruler
   Repeat the above instructions to place a vertical ruler guide at the **11cm** mark

3. Use the re-size pointer to reduce the width of the text frame.

   RESIZE

   RE-SIZE A TEXT FRAME
   Click on the text frame to highlight it
   Drag the *centre right handle* with the **Resize** pointer until the right margin of the text frame is in-line with the **10cm** vertical ruler guide (i.e. ½ the width it was)
   N.B. *At the bottom of the text frame a new button appears. This button indicates the text 'overflows' the frame.*

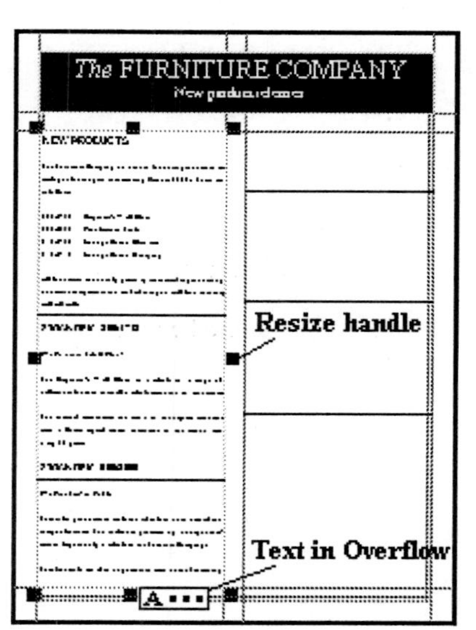

4. Select **Help**; **Microsoft Publisher Help**; choose the **Contents** tab; *double-click* the **Print Publications** book; *double-click* the **Text** book; *double-click* the **Add or replace text** book; *click* **Flow text from another text frame**. Select the What do you want to do? option **Connect text frames to flow text from one frame to another**. Read the Publisher Help screen carefully. **Close** the Publisher Help window.

5. Add a second text frame and placing the 'overflow' text in it.

CREATING A SECOND COLUMN OF TEXT
Click the **Text Frame Tool** on the left toolbar,
click in the left corner where the **5cm** horizontal guide meets the **11cm** vertical guide and hold and **drag** the mouse to where the the **28cm** horizontal guide meets the **20cm** vertical guide thus creating a *text frame*
ADDING THE TEXT OVERFLOW TO THE 2ND FRAME
Click on the *left text frame* to highlight it, select **Tools** and then **Connect Text Frames**, click the **Connect Text Frames** button on the toolbar

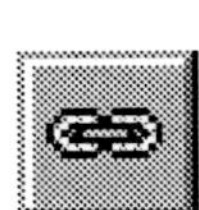

Click to **Pour** the text into the centre of the *right text frame*

6. Adjust the spacing between lines of text (leading).

ADJUSTING LINE SPACING (LEADING)
Click on the *left text frame* to highlight it
Select **Edit**, **Highlight Entire Story**, select **Format**, **Line Spacing**, type Between lines **12pt** and then click **OK**
N.B. *There should be NO change to the text.*
Select **Edit**, **Highlight Entire Story**, select **Format**, **Line Spacing**, type Between lines **18pt** and then click **OK**
N.B. *The text should fill out the frames.*

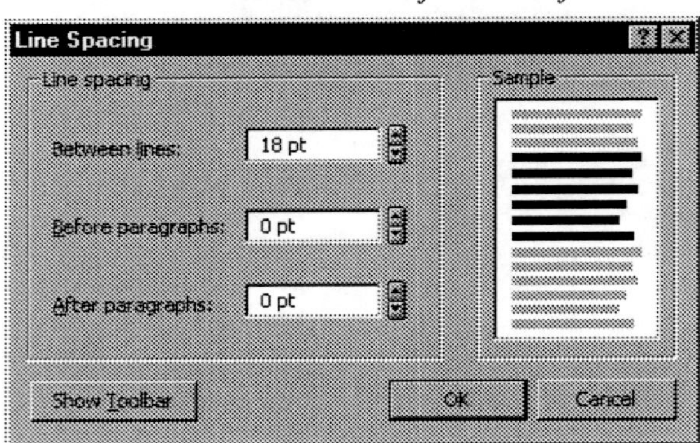

Select **Edit**, **Highlight Entire Story**, select **Format**, **Line Spacing**, type Between lines **24pt** and then click **OK**
Select **Edit**, **Highlight Entire Story**, select **Format**, **Line Spacing**, type Between lines **18pt** and then click **OK**
N.B. *This is the best fit at the moment because more text needs to be added.*

7. Enter the additional text (FURTHER DETAILS ....) at the end of the publication.

   ADDING FURTHER TEXT
   Click on the *right text frame* to highlight it
   Select **View**, **Zoom**, and then **100%**
   Type the text shown below at the end of the current text
   N.B. *Format the appropriate text as Bold. Set the Line Spacing to 18pt. Use the Shift* [⇧] *and Underscore* [_] *(between 0 and =) keys to draw the horizontal lines.*

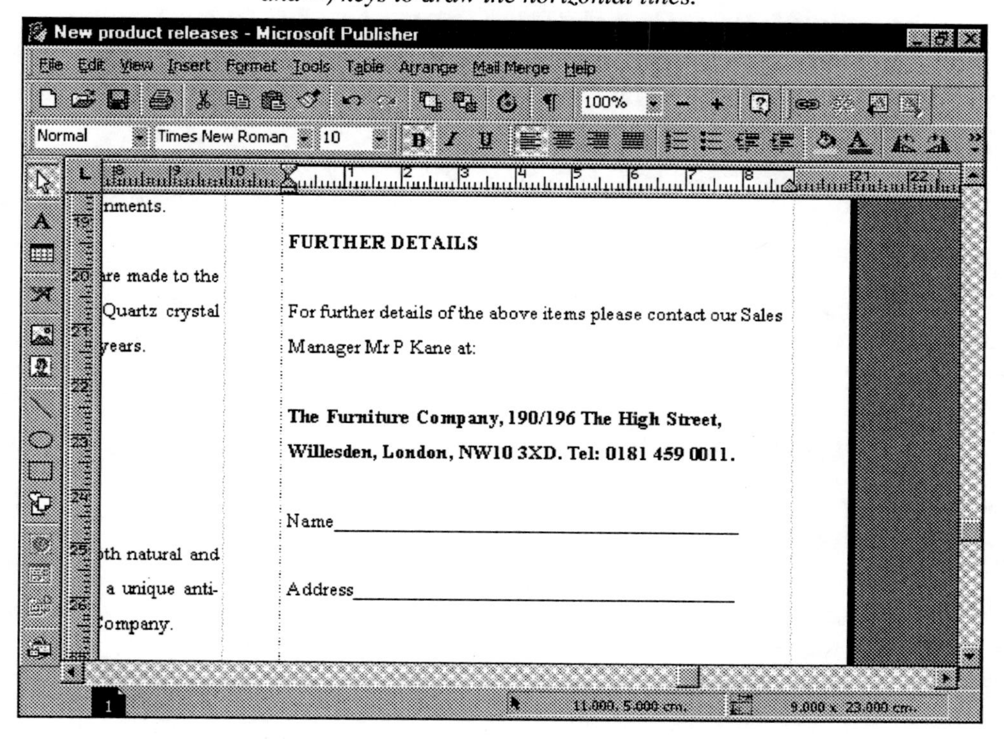

8. **Save** the changes made to the publication.

9. **Print** the publication.

10. Clear the publication by selecting **File** and then **Close**.

The FURNITURE COMPANY
New product releases

NEW PRODUCTS

The Furniture Company have added four new products to its catalogue for the year commencing October 1998. These are as follows:

256/1712 Carpenter's Wall Clock
600/2095 Pine Kitchen Table
645/1732 Lounge Unit in Black Ash
645/1749 Lounge Unit in Mahogany

All four items are keenly priced against similar products by our major competitors and we feel that you will find that they will sell well.

STOCK ITEM - 256/1712

The Carpenter's Wall Clock.

The Carpenter's Wall Clock is available in a range of different colours to suite all available tastes and environments.

The internal mechanisms are made to the highest standards with a Quartz crystal that is accurate to one second error every 10 years.

STOCK ITEM - 600/2095

The Pine Kitchen Table.

This solid pine kitchen table is available in both natural and antique finishes. A unique anti-scratch lacquer only available to The Furniture Company protects the surface.

This fine table can also be purchased with a set of matching chairs and would look at home in any dining room in the land.

STOCK ITEM - 645/1732

The Lounge Unit in Black Ash.

The Lounge Unit has a range of features that include four deep drawers and adjustable shelving which can vary from 6" to 20" in height. With its black ash textured finish this unit can be matched with the furnishings in most modern homes.

STOCK ITEM - 645/1749

The Lounge Unit in Mahogany.

This unit is the same as item 645/1732 as detailed above except that the finish is mahogany veneer. This unit has the same adjustable shelf features as the Lounge Unit in Black Ash.

FURTHER DETAILS

For further details of the above items please contact our Sales Manager Mr P Kane at:

The Furniture Company, 190/196 The High Street, Willesden, London, NW10 3XD. Tel: 0181 459 0011.

Name________________________________

Address______________________________

EXERCISE 15

OBJECTIVES

- To add a picture to a publication.
- To add lines to a publication.

INSTRUCTIONS

1. **Open** the publication called **NEW PRODUCT RELEASES.**

2. Insert a picture of the 'Carpenter's Wall Clock' to the left of the text.

   CREATING A PICTURE FRAME
   Select **View**, **Zoom**, and then **100%**
   Scroll Down the page until the details of the **'The Carpenter's Wall Clock'** are in view
   Click the **Picture Frame Tool** on the left toolbar,
   create a **3cm** by **3cm** *picture frame* against the left border approximately from the 18cm to 21cm mark on the vertical ruler
   N.B. *The text should be displaced.*
   INSERTING A PICTURE IN THE FRAME
   N.B. *The picture frame must be highlighted - that is the 8 boxes (handles) should be showing.*
   Select **Insert**, **Picture**, and then **From File**
   Highlight the **3 ½ Floppy (A:)** folder in the Look in box
   Type **Clock** in the File name box
   Click **Insert** to place the picture

3. Draw lines, of thickness 4pt, between each of the sections.

   DRAWING LINES
   Select **Tools** and place a tick ☑ against **Snap to Guides**
   Scroll Down the page until the details of the **'The Carpenter's Wall Clock'** are in view
   Click the **Line** button on the left toolbar, just above the text **STOCK ITEM - 256/1712** draw a horizontal line from the **1cm** vertical guide to the **10cm** vertical guide, Select **Format**, **Line/Border Style**, select **More Styles...**, select Line thickness **4pt**, and then **OK**
   Repeat this by drawing a further 4 lines just above **STOCK ITEM - 600/2095**, **STOCK ITEM - 645/1732**, **STOCK ITEM - 645/1749** and **FURTHER DETAILS**

4. **Save** the changes made to the publication.

5. **Print** the publication.

6. Clear the publication by selecting **File** and then **Close**.

The FURNITURE COMPANY

New product releases

NEW PRODUCTS

The Furniture Company have added four new products to its catalogue for the year commencing October 1998. These are as follows:

256/1712 Carpenter's Wall Clock
600/2095 Pine Kitchen Table
645/1732 Lounge Unit in Black Ash
645/1749 Lounge Unit in Mahogany

All four items are keenly priced against similar products by our major competitors and we feel that you will find that they will sell well.

STOCK ITEM - 256/1712

The Carpenter's Wall Clock.

The Carpenter's Wall Clock is available in a range of different colours to suite all available tastes and environments.

The internal mechanisms are made to the highest standards with a Quartz crystal that is accurate to one second error every 10 years.

STOCK ITEM - 600/2095

The Pine Kitchen Table.

This solid pine kitchen table is available in both natural and antique finishes. A unique anti-scratch lacquer only available to The Furniture Company protects the surface.

This fine table can also be purchased with a set of matching chairs and would look at home in any dining room in the land.

STOCK ITEM - 645/1732

The Lounge Unit in Black Ash.

The Lounge Unit has a range of features that include four deep drawers and adjustable shelving which can vary from 6" to 20" in height. With its black ash textured finish this unit can be matched with the furnishings in most modern homes.

STOCK ITEM - 645/1749

The Lounge Unit in Mahogany.

This unit is the same as item 645/1732 as detailed above except that the finish is mahogany veneer. This unit has the same adjustable shelf features as the Lounge Unit in Black Ash.

FURTHER DETAILS

For further details of the above items please contact our Sales Manager Mr P Kane at:

The Furniture Company, 190/196 The High Street, Willesden, London, NW10 3XD. Tel: 0181 459 0011.

Name________________________________

Address______________________________

EXERCISE 16

OBJECTIVES

- Producing a simple Flyer.
- Using Landscape mode.

INSTRUCTIONS

1. Open a new publication.

   OPENING A NEW PUBLICATION
   Select **File** and then **New**
   THEN/OR
   From the Catalog screen choose the **Blank Publications** tab
   THEN
   Select the type of publication you want to create as a **Full Page** publication (in either the left or right window), and then click **Create**

2. Set the page for landscape mode.

   USING LANDSCAPE MODE
   Select **File**, **Page Setup**, Choose an Orientation **Landscape**, then click **OK**

3. Set the page margin guides of the new publication.

   SETTING THE PAGE MARGIN GUIDES
   Select **Arrange**, **Layout Guides**, change the Left, Right, Top and Bottom Margin Guides to **2 cm**, and then click **OK**

4. Create horizontal ruler guides at 5cm, 10cm, and 15cm from the top of the page.

   CREATING HORIZONTAL RULER GUIDES
   Select **View** and tick ☑ the **Rulers** option
   Hold down the **Shift** ⇧ key and point at the *horizontal* ruler until the **Adjust** pointer appears, click and **drag** the mouse to place a horizontal dashed line on the publication against the **5cm** mark on the *vertical* ruler
   Repeat the above instructions to place horizontal ruler guides at the **10cm**, and **15cm** marks

5. Create a vertical ruler guide 15cm from the left of the page.

CREATING VERTICAL RULER GUIDES

Hold down the **Shift** ⇧ key and point at the *vertical* ruler until the **Adjust** pointer appears, click and **drag** the mouse to place a vertical dashed line on the publication against the **15cm** mark on the *horizontal* ruler

6. Enter the company's address, placing it accurately on the page.

CREATING A TEXT FRAME

Click the **Text Frame Tool** A on the left toolbar, click in the left corner where the **15cm** horizontal guide meets the **2cm** left margin guide and hold and **drag** the mouse to the lower right corner where the **19cm** bottom margin guide meets the **15cm** vertical guide thus creating a *text frame*

FORMATTING AND ENTERING TEXT IN A TEXT FRAME

Click the **Bold** B button, click the **Center** text button, select **View**, **Zoom**, and then **100%**, type the text:

190/196 The High Street
Willesden
London
NW10 3XD
Tel: 0181 459 0011
Fax: 0181 459 0022

Select **View**, **Zoom**, and then **Whole Page**

7. Enter the text 'THE FURNITURE COMPANY', placing it accurately on the page.

CREATING A TEXT FRAME

Click the **Text Frame Tool** A on the left toolbar, click in the left corner where the **5cm** horizontal guide meets the **15cm** vertical guide and hold and **drag** the mouse to the lower right corner margin where the **10cm** horizontal guide meets the **28cm** right margin guide thus creating a *text frame*

FORMATTING AND ENTERING TEXT IN A TEXT FRAME

Select a Font Size **24**pt, click the **Bold** B button, click the **Center** text button, type the text N.B. *Include spaces between each character*:

T H E
F U R N I T U R E
C O M P A N Y

8. **Save** the publication with the File name **FLYER 1**.

9. **Print** the publication.

10. Clear the publication by selecting **File** and then **Close**.

THE

FURNITURE

COMPANY

190/196 The High Street
Willesden
London
NW10 3XD
Tel: 0181 459 0011
Fax: 0181 459 0022

EXERCISE 17

OBJECTIVES

- Producing a simple flyer.
- Using Landscape mode.
- Using the Oval and Line tools.

INSTRUCTIONS

1. **Open** the publication **FLYER 1**.
2. Delete the text in the two text boxes.
3. Type in the text as shown over the page in the right hand box.
4. Add a Oval around the outside of the text.

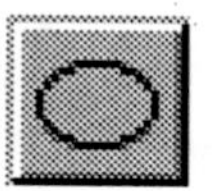

ADDING AN OVAL SHAPE
Click the **Oval Tool** on the drawing toolbar
Click to the *top left* of the text and **drag** the pointer to the *bottom right* of the text - adjust the size of the oval to fit around the text

5. Add 4 lines from the oval to the margin borders.

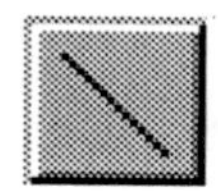

ADDING LINES
Click the **Line Tool** on the drawing toolbar
Click in the left corner where the **5cm** horizontal guide meets the **15cm** vertical guide and hold and **drag** the mouse to meet the Oval to the left of Trade Day
Repeat this for the other 3 lines joining where the margin guides meet to the Oval as shown

6. Use the Save As command to save a publication with a different name.

USING SAVE AS
Select **File**, **Save As**, type the File name **FLYER 2**, and then click to **Save** the file

7. **Print** the publication.
8. Place the publications FLYER 1 and FLYER 2 back to back and then fold in two to create the invite.
9. Clear the publication by selecting **File** and then **Close**.

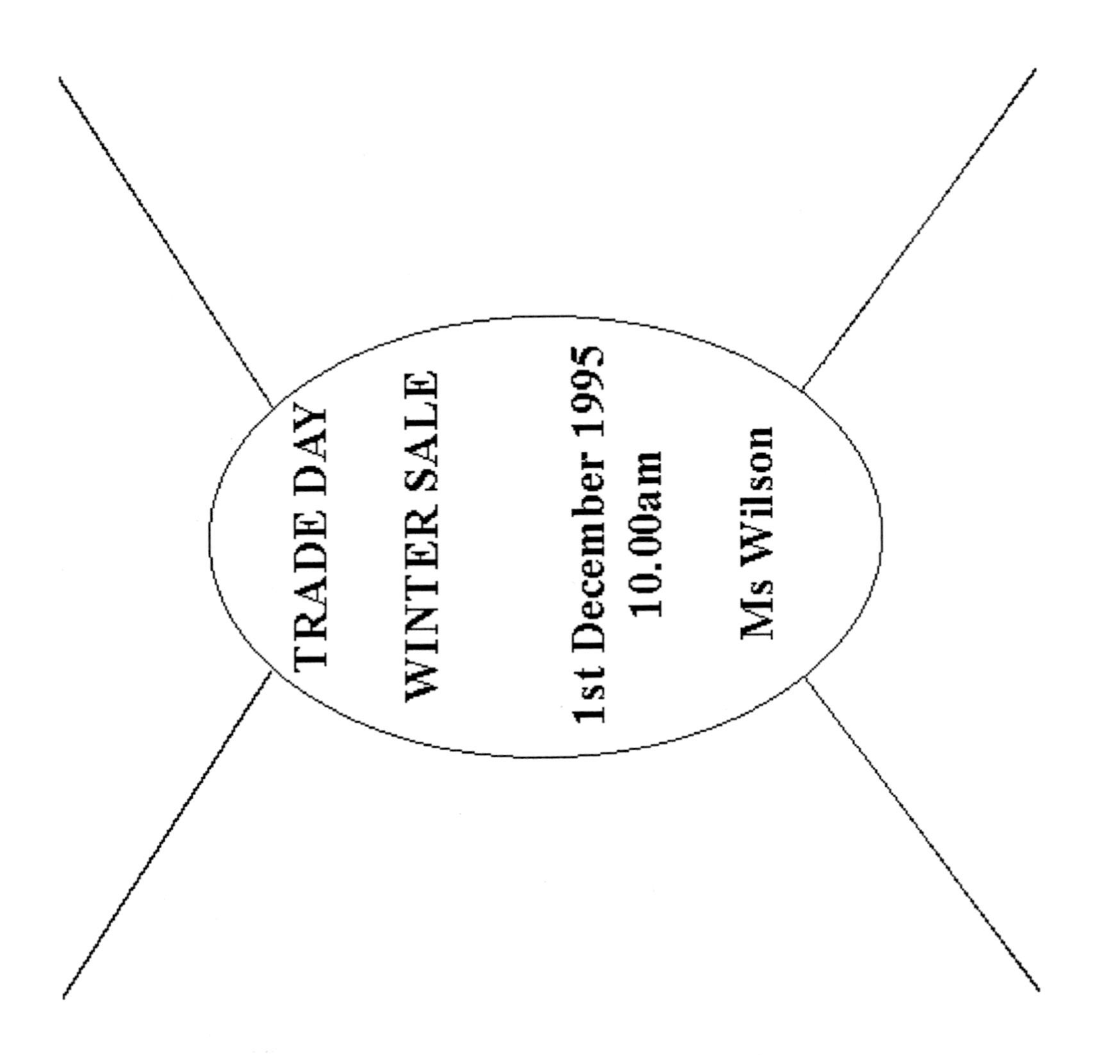
TRADE DAY
WINTER SALE
1st December 1995
10.00am
Ms Wilson

EXERCISE 18

OBJECTIVES

- Producing a Newsletter using a Wizard.

INSTRUCTIONS

1. Open a new publication using the Newsletter Wizard.

   OPENING A NEW PUBLICATION USING A WIZARD
   Select **File** and then **New**
   THEN/OR
   From the Catalog screen choose the **Publications by Wizard** tab
   THEN
   In the Wizards window select **Newsletters**, in the Newsletters window highlight the **Arcs Newsletter** publication, then click the **Start Wizard** button

2. Set up the page by answering the Wizard's questions.

   CREATING THE PAGE
   Click **OK** to tell the wizard about yourself
   Edit the details requested
   N.B. *These details will only be asked the first time the wizard is run.*

3. Replace the "Lead Story Headline" with the name of the **Course** you are studying/have studied. Below the new title write an article about your course (highlight and delete the existing text).

4. Replace the "Secondary Story Headline" with **Information Technology at the college**. Below the new title write an article about Information Technology that you have studied on your course.

5. Replace the text in the other boxes on the page with some further details about your college or some special event on at the college in the near future. Change the picture and other headings as necessary.

6. **Save** the publication with the File name **College Newsletter**.

7. **Print** the publication.

8. Clear the publication by selecting **File** and then **Close**.

EXERCISE 19

OBJECTIVES

- Producing a Brochure using a Wizard.
- Creating an Encapsulated PostScript (EPS) file.

INSTRUCTIONS

1. Open a new publication using the Brochure Wizard.

   OPENING A NEW PUBLICATION USING A WIZARD
   Select **File** and then **New**
   THEN/OR
   From the Catalog screen choose the **Publications by Wizard** tab
   THEN
   In the Wizards window select **Brochures** and **Informational**, in the Informational Brochures window highlight the **Bars Informational Brochure** publication, then click the **Start Wizard** button

2. Edit the right (front cover) panel of the brochure.

   EDITING TEXT
   Select **View**, **Zoom**, and then **100%**
   Use the **Scroll Left/Right** ◄ ► buttons to scroll the screen to the right panel
   The company name should read **The Furniture Company**, and the brochure title should read **Product/Service Information**
   Replace *Your business tag line here* with **Taking care of your needs**
   REPLACING THE COMPANY LOGO
   Highlight the building **logo** that appears below *Taking care of your needs*
   Select **Insert**, **Picture**, and then **From File**
   Highlight the **3 ½ Floppy (A:)** folder in the Look in box
   Type **Real Estate** in the File name box
   Click **Insert** to place the picture
   EDITING TEXT
   Highlight the telephone number and replace it with **Tel: 0181 459 0011**

3. Edit the centre panel of the brochure.

   EDITING TEXT
   The company name should read **The Furniture Company**, with the address **190/196 The High Street, Willesden, London, NW10 3XD**
   Enter the Phone number **0181 459 0011**
   Enter the Fax number **0181 459 0022**
   Delete the Email details

4. Edit the left panel of the brochure.

   EDITING TEXT
   Replace the *Back Panel Heading* with **Product/Service Information**
   Highlight the text box below this new heading and enter the text **All items supplied by The Furniture Company come with a 30 day no fuss money back guarantee**

5. **Save** the publication with the File name **BROCHURE**.

6. **Print** the publication.

7. Select **Help**; **Microsoft Publisher Help**; choose the **Contents** tab; *double-click* the **Print Publications** book; *double-click* the **Printing topics for printing professionals** book; *click* **Create an Encapsulated PostScript (EPS) file based on your publication**. Read the Publisher Help screen carefully. **Close** the Publisher Help window.

POSTSCRIPT

Commercial printing services usually require files to be saved in Postscript or Encapsulated PostScript format, hence the file extension .EPS is used here.

If your system does not have a Postscript driver installed you will need to install one.

8. Create Encapsulated PostScript (EPS) files for each of the 2 pages of this brochure. N.B. *This will only work if you have a PostScript driver installed on your system.*

   SETTING THE COLOUR OPTION TO USE
   Select **Tool**, **Commercial Printing Tools**, **Color Printing**, set to Print all colors as **Composite RGB** and then click **OK**
   SETTING THE PRINTING TO EPS FORMAT
   Select **View** and then remove the tick ☐ from **Two-Page Spread**
   Select **File**, **Print Setup**, set the printer Name to any **PostScript printer PS** on your system, click **Properties**, set the PostScript output format to **Encapsulated PostScript (EPS)**, then click **OK**, **OK**, and **OK**
   PRINTING AN EPS FILE TO DISC FOR PAGE 1
   Click the **Page 1** [1] tab at the bottom of the screen
   Select **File**, **Print**, set the Print range to **Current page**, tick ☑ to **Print to file**, click **OK** to print, type the File name **Brochure1.EPS** and again click **OK**
   PRINTING AN EPS FILE TO DISC FOR PAGE 2
   Click the **Page 2** [2] tab at the bottom of the screen
   Select **File**, **Print**, set the Print range to **Current page**, tick ☑ to **Print to file**, click **OK** to print, type the File name **Brochure2.EPS** and again click **OK**

9. Clear the publication by selecting **File** and then **Close**.

Product/ Service
Information

All items supplied by The Furniture Company come

with a 30 day no fuss money back guarantee.

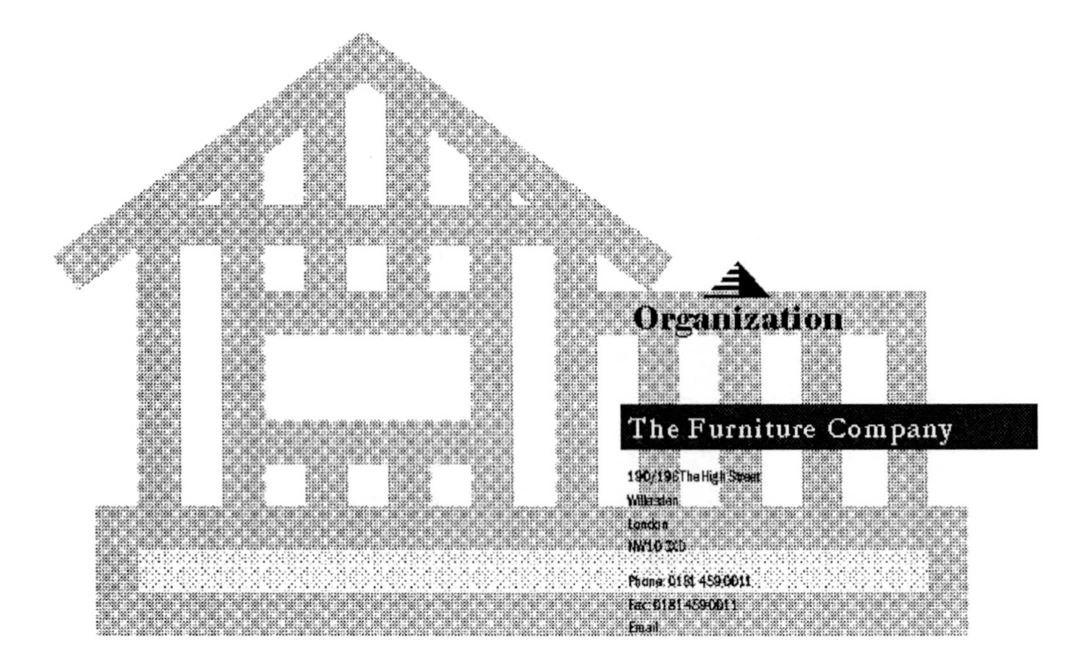

Taking care of your needs.

Tel: 0181 459 0011

ADDITIONAL EXERCISES

ADDITIONAL EXERCISE 1

1. Open a new publication and set the margins to 3cm on all sides.
2. Create a single-line border, of line-thickness 4pt, along the margins of the publication.
3. Type the heading “FLAG” at the top of the publication using an Arial font, size 24pt, centred, and made bold.
4. Import the picture file ‘Flag’ from your floppy disc and place it in 4 frames as shown over the page. Use flip/rotate/mirror as appropriate.
5. Save the publication with the file name FLAG-1.

F
L
A
G

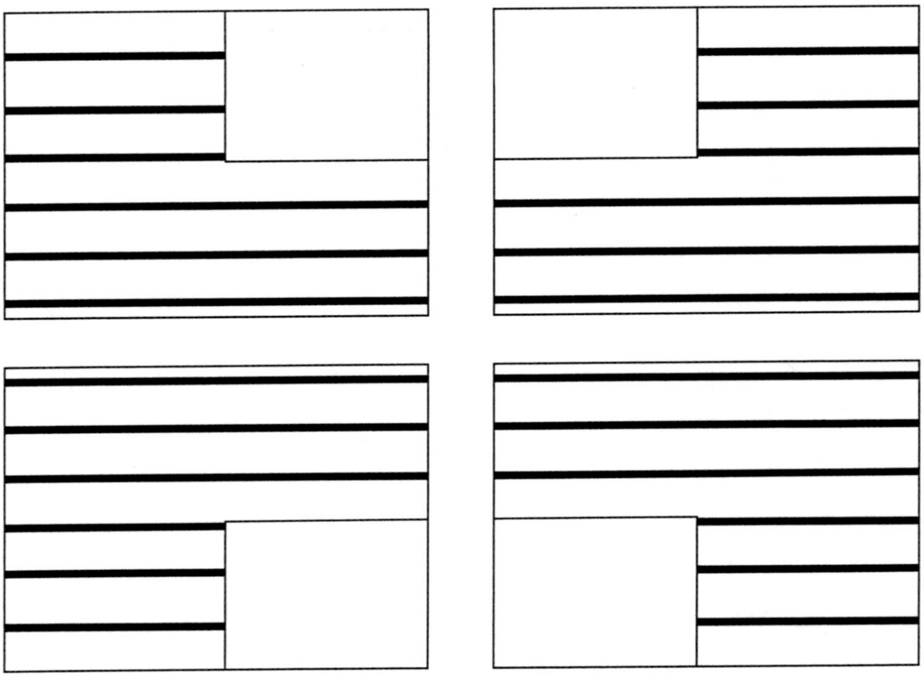

ADDITIONAL EXERCISE 2

1. Open a new publication and set the margins to 3cm on all sides.
2. Create a double-line border, of line-thickness 2pt, along the margins of the publication.
3. Type the heading "FLAG" at the top of the publication using an Arial font, size 24pt, centred, and made bold.
4. Type the sub-heading "Cropped" at the top of the publication using an Arial font, size 20pt, centred, and made bold and italic.
5. Import the picture file 'Flag' from your floppy disc and place it in frames as shown over the page. Use crop/flip/rotate as appropriate.
6. Save the publication with the file name FLAG-2.

F
L
A
G

Cropped

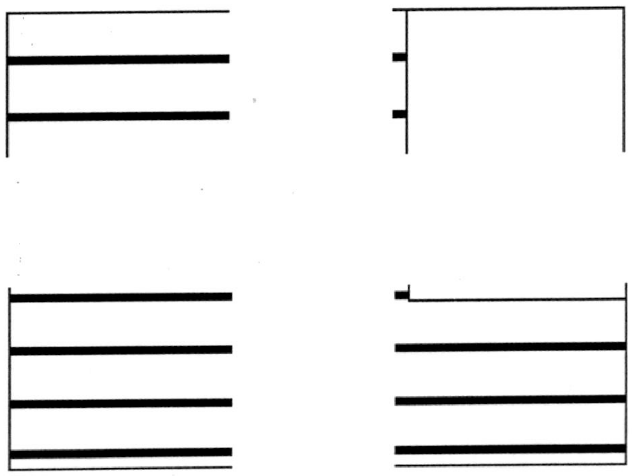

ADDITIONAL EXERCISE 3

1. Open the publication FLAG-1.
2. Change the border to double-line, of thickness 2pt, along the margins of the publication.
3. Type the sub-heading "With diamonds" at the top of the publication using an Arial font, size 20pt, centred, and made bold and italic.
4. Edit the picture 'Flag' in the frames to include the "diamonds". Use a pixel editor to do this.
5. Save the publication with the new file name FLAG-3.

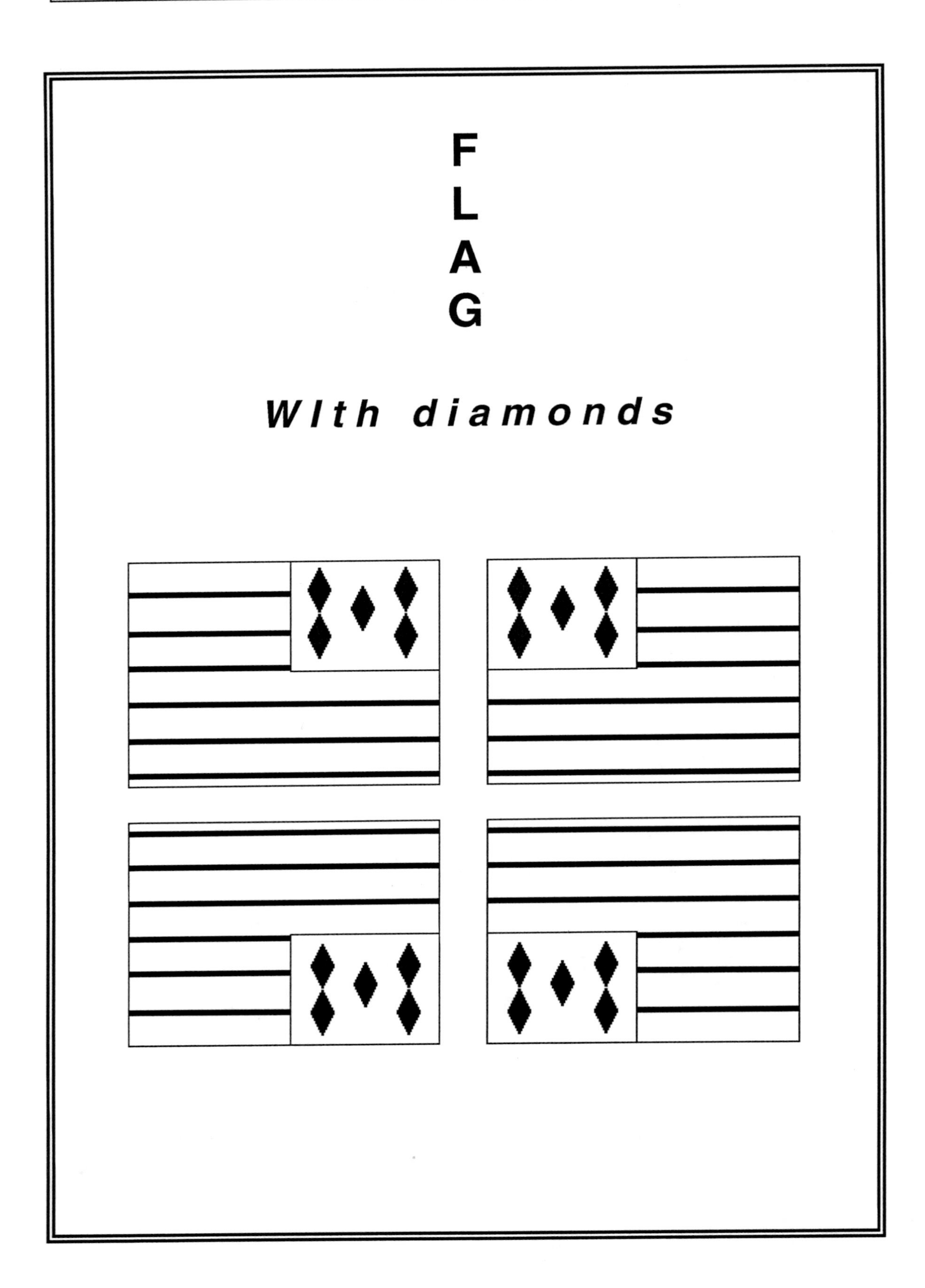
F
L
A
G
WIth diamonds

ADDITIONAL EXERCISE 4

1. Open a new publication and set the margins to 2cm on all sides.
2. Set the orientation of the page as portrait.
3. Import the text files 'Art Deco' and 'Luggage' from your floppy disc and place the text as shown using appropriate fonts and styles. Type in the additional text as required.
4. Use the line tool to add appropriate lines to the publication.
5. Import the clip-art files 'Art Deco' and 'Luggage' from your floppy disc and place them in appropriate frames as shown over the page.
6. Save the publication with the file name ADVERT.

The Furniture Company

1998/99 Sales Catalogue - New Product Lines

The latest additions to our product range are a number of household items in the Art Deco style. These include:

- Table lighting.
- Mirrors.
- Coffee tables.

These items are only available at *The Furniture Company* having been commissioned from an internationally renowned designer.

LUGGAGE

We are pleased to offer in our latest catalogue a new range of goods never before sold *by The Furniture Company*. A range of high quality holiday luggage at sensible prices has been added to our latest catalogue. For a limited period only all of this luggage range will be available with a 25% discount.

For further information and a copy of our latest catalogue please contact:
The Furniture Company, 190/196 The High Street, Willesden, London, NW10 3XD.
Tel: 0181 459 0011. Fax: 0181 459 0022.

ADDITIONAL EXERCISE 5

1. Open a new publication and set the margins to 1cm on all sides.
2. Set the orientation of the page as landscape.
3. Import the picture file 'Computer User' from your floppy disc and place it in a frame as shown over the page.
4. Type in the text as shown using appropriate fonts and styles.
5. Use the line drawing tool to create the various lines shown.
6. Save the publication with the file name CATALOGUE-1.

Software Training Workbooks

for students on

Computing Courses

The workbooks are suitable for use on a range of Computing and IT Courses.

The workbooks are also ideally suited for use in Open Learning Resource Centres.

For further information please contact:

Software Training Workbooks

I would like further details:

Name ____________________

Department ____________________

Address ____________________

____

Post Code __________ **Tel:** __________

ADDITIONAL EXERCISE 6

1. Open a new publication and set the margins to 1cm on all sides.

2. Set the orientation of the page as landscape.

3. Import the picture file 'Graph' from your floppy disc and place it in an appropriate frame as shown over the page.

4. Import the text file 'Workbooks' and place the text as shown using appropriate fonts and styles. Type in and/or edit the additional text/headings as required.

5. Use the line drawing tool to create the line shown.

6. Save the publication with the file name CATALOGUE-2.

... Level 2 Workbooks

Word 97 for Windows - Level 2

These workbooks have been written to follow on from the Introduction to Word 97 workbooks also available from STW.

The exercises are centred around creating house-style business letters, writing memos, writing reports, producing marketing and advertising material, and developing financial forms.

Excel 97 for Windows - Level 2

These workbooks have been written to follow on from the Introduction to Excel 97 workbooks also available from STW.

The exercises include using Forms, using Max/Min/Count functions, using IF statements, protecting and un-protecting cells, using the Hide commands, importing & exporting data, producing abstract reports which include headers, footers, borders and shading, setting print areas, and also there is an introduction to simple Macros.

... Level 2 Workbooks

Access 97 for Windows - Level 2

These workbooks have been written to follow on from the Introduction to Access 97 workbooks also available from STW with the same Company database used as the basis for the exercises.

The first part of the workbook includes exercises on designing forms, looking at table properties and structures, advanced querying, and producing reports.

DEBTORS SCHEDULE (JAN-MAR)

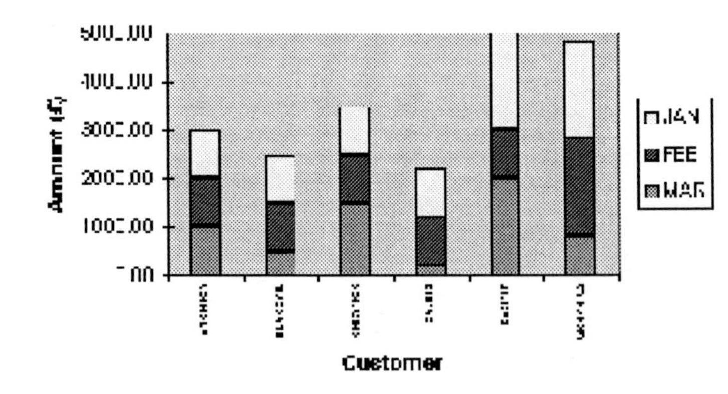

TOOLBARS - Standard/Formatting (Text/Table Frame)

- New
- Open
- Save
- Print
- Cut
- Copy
- Paste
- Format Painter
- Undo
- Redo
- Bring to Front
- Send to Back
- Custom Rotate
- Show Special Characters
- 27% Zoom
- Zoom Out
- Zoom In
- Microsoft Publisher Help

- Normal Style
- Times New Roman Font
- 10 Font Size
- Bold
- Italic
- Underline
- Align Left
- Center
- Align Right
- Justify
- Numbering
- Bullets
- Decrease Indent
- Increase Indent
- Decrease Font Size
- Increase Font Size
- Fill Color
- Line Color
- Font Color
- Line/Border Style
- Text Frame/Table Cell Properties
- Rotate Left
- Rotate Right
- More Buttons

TOOLBARS - Formatting (WordArt/ClipArt/Picture/Object)

Crop Picture

Flip Horizontal

Flip Vertical

Wrap Text to Frame

Wrap Text to Picture

Object Properties

TOOLBARS - Drawing

Pointer Tool

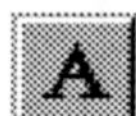
Text Frame Tool

Table Frame Tool

WordArt Frame Tool

Picture Frame Tool

Clip Gallery Tool

Line Tool

Oval Tool

Rectangle Tool

Custom Shapes

Hot Spot Tool

Form Control

HTML Code Fragment

Design Gallery Object

GRAPHICS FILES

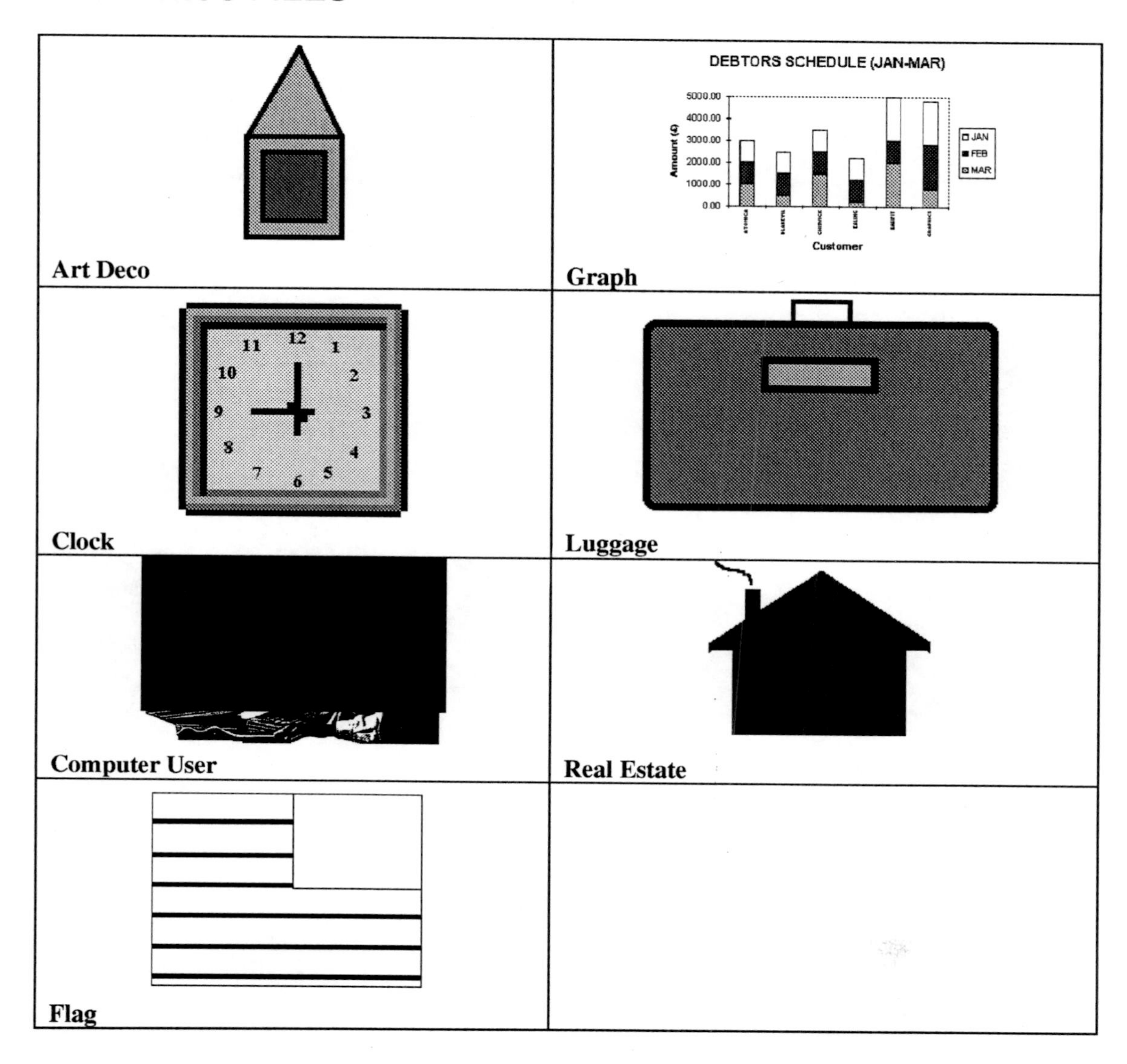